KT-508-922

REAKTHROUGH TO LITERACY

BREAKTHROUGH TO LITERACY

Teacher's Manual

The theory and practice of
teaching initial reading and writing

David Mackay, Brian Thompson and
Pamela Schaub

Schools Council Programme in Linguistics
and English Teaching
Director: M. A. K. Halliday
Communication Research Centre
Department of General Linguistics
University College London

Longman for the Schools Council

To all the teachers and children
who helped us in writing this book

LONGMAN FOR THE SCHOOLS COUNCIL

LONGMAN GROUP LIMITED
London

Associated companies, branches and representatives
throughout the world

© Schools Council Publications 1970

All rights reserved. No part of this publication may be
reproduced, stored in a retrieval system, or transmitted
in any form or by any means, electronic, mechanical,
photocopying, recording, or otherwise, without
the prior permission of the Copyright owner.

First published 1970
Fifth impression 1973

ISBN 0 582 19060 6

Printed in Hong Kong by
Peninsula Press Ltd

FOREWORD

M. A. K. Halliday

Breakthrough to Literacy is the work of the 'Initial Literacy project', which is part of the Programme in Linguistics and English Teaching at University College London. The Initial Literacy project consists of a small independent team led by David Mackay, formerly Headmaster of Beatrix Potter Primary School in London. His ideas and those of his colleague Brian Thompson have been the main source of inspiration. But far from being an isolated venture, their work has formed an essential part of the search for an integrated, strategic approach to the learning of the mother tongue at all levels throughout the school; a search for a better understanding of how children can be helped towards linguistic success, without which they cannot achieve success in school at all.

It would be impossible to give in a few sentences a balanced account of the principles underlying the *Breakthrough* materials; this is, after all, what the present Manual is about. But one of the things that has impressed me in seeing *Breakthrough* at work has been the co-operation that it engenders among the children who are using it. One child will recognize which step it is that another is finding difficult – it may be one he has recently taken himself – and will spontaneously interfere and explain. He explains it, of course, in his own way, which is probably not the way in which you or I would have thought of explaining it. But the language he uses is appropriate to the situation, and we can learn a lot from observing what he says.

In a sense this collaboration of teacher and learner (for that is what it is) is symbolic of the collaboration that lies behind the work itself; collaboration, in this case, among teachers, at primary, secondary and university levels. This also has involved quite a lot of translating and interpreting. The language of research in linguistics, psychology or sociology is not the same as the language of infant teaching; this is inevitable – they are activities of quite different kinds. But this is not to say that the different specialists cannot learn to talk to each other. In any case it is a mistake to think that the university teacher comes into the picture only as a research worker; he is also, first and foremost, a teacher, and in this role he is on the same wavelength as his colleagues from infant class to sixth form. The difficulties of communication within the Programme have by no means always reflected the dividing line between school and university; sometimes the language barrier has been between primary and secondary, and sometimes there has been a ready understanding between the university members and their primary school colleagues not shared by those whose experience lay in between.

The Programme has attempted to put all these components together and look at the whole problem of language in school, taking account not only of the basic skills of reading and writing and the traditional concerns of the teacher of 'subject English' but also of the demands made on the child's language potential by the school as a whole, and by the community at large. The influence of this wider context is very clearly seen in the present Manual; the child has to learn to read and write, but the concept of 'initial literacy' is much broader and much more closely linked to the child's total experience of language, as it is at the time and as it will be in the years to come.

So we tend to take a functional view of language, thinking primarily of what the child can do with language and how it can enrich his life. Most children, even by the time they first come to school, although there is a great deal of their mother tongue which they still have to learn, yet have mastered a rich variety of uses for what they do know. Unless what they are doing in school relates to the uses of language with which they are familiar, and makes sense in terms of what they need language for, it will not carry them far. This concern with the child's experience of language, and his linguistic needs, is evident throughout the Manual: in the emphasis on the spoken language, in the references to the language of imagination and play, and in many other ways.

But there are children who have not had this variety of linguistic experience, and who will not get it outside the school; for them the teacher, and the teacher's specialist skill and knowledge are the only hope of linguistic success. Do not think that the supporting activities – talking with this specialist about language, and, with her active help, investigating the mysteries of writing – are just optional extras for the favoured ones. On the contrary, these are the foundations of success, and it is those children whom the chances are most against who need in particular to talk about and to understand what they are trying to do. In all his other learning activities, the child talks about what he is learning as he goes along; why should language be an exception? As those who helped with the trials well know, there has been considerable emphasis on the needs of those who are most likely to fail; and it is particularly in helping these children that the teacher's own understanding of the nature and functions of language plays an essential part.

A number of different bodies contributed to the resources that made this work possible. The Nuffield Foundation provided the grant that started off the research, and the Department of Education and Science supplemented this by paying for the teachers to participate. This was Stage I (1964–1967). The Schools Council then took over and financed the whole of Stage II (1967–1970). The work has been done in the University of London. The Communication Research Centre, which itself received a grant from the Longman Group Limited, is part of the Department of General Linguistics at University College London; the College has provided accommodation and office services, and the team has taken full advantage of the teaching and research facilities provided by this and other departments. But there is much more to any project than the money that went into it. There is the wealth of knowledge and experience drawn from all those associated with it: our colleagues at University College and at the London Institute of Education, the staff of other Institutes and Colleges of Education up and down the country, the specialist inspectors and advisers – and most of all the many teachers in the trial areas who have used the material, pulled it apart, put it together again and, in a positive sense, 'given us a piece of their minds'. I hope they will find that their generosity has not been wasted.

M. A. K. Halliday

Communication Research Centre
Department of General Linguistics
University College London

CONTENTS

PART ONE: THE MATERIALS

INTRODUCTION

The first part of this teacher's book[1] is intended as a practical guide to the use of the *Breakthrough to literacy* materials in the classroom. We do not at any stage indicate how long the work discussed in this book should take a child; nor do we state at what age or at what time in the school year a child should start using the materials. They are intended to be used individually by children working at their own pace. A few children may have only just started this work by the end of their first year in the Infant School while other children have made great progress in their ability to use written language before the year is out. Such differences are quite normal and there should be no pressure on the children to complete the work outlined here in their first year at school. The children who begin to learn to read later than their peers may catch up in the following year and, in the Junior School, equal or surpass them.

What we are offering here is not wholly new and revolutionary. Many of the ideas outlined in the following pages refer to things that good Infants' School teachers are already doing. What we have tried to do is to examine current practices and to attempt to work out why certain procedures are successful and others less so. Some of the practices used in the teaching of reading may well be found to have little value. The sets of matching exercises that involve pictures of clowns' faces,

---

[1] Much of the material for this book is taken from the Manual that accompanied the trial materials and from part of the paper *The Initial Teaching of Reading and Writing: some notes towards a Theory of Literacy* (Mackay and Thompson). New material has been added as a result of teachers' comments and criticisms.

animals and flowers, for example, may be pleasant games, but it has yet to be shown that they affect in any way at all the child's ability to notice similarities and differences in written words. Perhaps the most crucial difference between *Breakthrough to literacy* and reading schemes currently available is the way we have set out aspects of the teaching and learning of literacy and linked these within an overall framework.

Because we believe the method of marking progress in reading by reference to the page number in a series of books is misleading and uninformative, we have replaced it with an explicit and carefully graded description of the chief processes involved in learning to read and write.

The Sentence Maker is designed to overcome two major difficulties that small children have when they attempt to write: their lack of manual dexterity in handling a writing tool and the difficulty they have in spelling words. The Sentence Maker presents the child with bits of language already printed so that his task is to learn to arrange these to compose sentences. Handwriting and spelling are not neglected. They are taught as skills separate from that of composing a written text.

Unlike traditional reading schemes *Breakthrough to literacy* integrates the production (writing) and the reception (reading) of written language. When the child is learning to speak he is involved in both the production (speaking) and the reception (listening) of spoken language; but when he comes to learn to read and write he is introduced to the receptive skill, reading, before the productive skill, writing. This is largely because it is difficult for him to produce written language unaided. The Sentence Maker is designed to allow him to do just this.

Some of the other fundamental beliefs underlying *Breakthrough to literacy* are that:

1 Reading matter for children should, from the beginning, be linked to their own spoken language. The child's neighbourhood dialect may well be the only resource he brings to learning to read and write, and to present him with written language unrelated to his spoken language is to cut him off from this. The language of

most reading books, especially most first books, is very different from the spoken language of children and adults and includes sentences not found in normal written English.

2 The material that children are asked to read should be closely linked to their own interests and experiences and should include forms of imaginative writing.

3 The teacher should be an active participant in the child's learning process, constantly offering the child guidance and help. Language, spoken and written, is highly patterned and the more of this patterning the teacher understands the more effectively will she be able to help children to learn to read and write.

Breakthrough to literacy: a list of the materials

Teacher's Materials

Teacher's Sentence Maker, Stand, printed inserts and blank inserts

Teacher's Magnet Board Kit: magnet board, a set of cards of figurines and magnets

Manual

Children's materials

Sentence Maker, Stand, printed inserts and blank inserts

Word Maker, printed inserts

Breakthrough books

after school	In bed
big and little	The Christmas tree
the cat, the bird and the tree	Birds
a fish book	Shopping
my mum	The birthday party
I fell over	Dressing up
a cup of tea	Doctors and nurses
things I can do	The loose tooth
at school	The lost girl
my teacher	People in stories
a rainy day	My story
the wendy house	Our baby

Big breakthrough books

An abc for hungry girls and boys
About the house

Nursery rhyme materials

Sally go round the sun and other nursery rhymes,
cards and accompanying record

Additional equipment you may find useful

A Teacher's Model of the Word Maker (directions are
given in this manual for the making of this item).
Charts for Weather, Number and Colour. (We have
included directions and plans of possible models of
these in the manual.)
Simple reading books, picture story books, nursery
rhyme books and reference books for teachers as
detailed in the appendices to this manual.

1

BEGINNING

Introducing the children to written language

Before the children begin to work with the Sentence Maker and the Word Maker, they have much to learn about written language. We take so much for granted when we read and write that it is very difficult for us to realize how complicated a task it is for small children.

Many children arrive at school with little idea of what written language is; some children may not understand the difference between the text and the illustrations in a picture story book, nor the connection between the marks on the page and the words spoken aloud by the teacher when she reads stories. Even though our children are surrounded by written language in shops, on the television screen, in the streets, in magazines, newspapers and books, it remains for most of them a mysterious code and they have no clue as to how to decipher it.

At first you should read to the children from picture story books and discuss with them precisely what you are doing, helping them to understand the difference between *reading* a story and *telling* a story. Children should be encouraged to discuss the differences between the text and the picture. They sometimes think that the line of print under illustrations is no more than a decorative border.

Next the connection between the printed marks and spoken language should be established by saying something like 'these marks show me what I must say'. If you say 'This word says . . . ' or 'This letter says . . .' make sure that children understand that you are speaking figuratively (since the written marks do not and cannot *say* anything).

Another aspect of the writing system that should be dealt with at this time is the directionality of written

English. When you are reading show children that you start at the top left hand corner and read each line from left to right, from the top line to the bottom, following the lines of print with your finger to show the direction. Large wall charts of nursery rhymes are particularly easy to follow and establish this point well.

Children hear and think of spoken language as continuous sound. The nursery rhyme cards are useful in this connection; if you point to the words while reading the rhyme and draw the children's attention to the word spaces, they will begin to identify words as separate units.

In discussing how and what we read, encourage children to think about these things for themselves by asking questions such as 'Where is the first piece of writing on this page?', show them a page of illustration and ask 'Can I read this page?'. The children's own questions and answers will help you to see what they have not yet understood. It is possible to introduce the idea of a word by reading or saying a very short sentence and then asking 'How many words was that?'.

All writings put up round the room (see 'Notices in the classroom') help to reinforce knowledge about written language but they need to be brought to children's attention frequently.

Language to talk about language

In the course of all the discussion about written language the children will be learning the meaning of words such as *listening, speaking, reading, telling, sound, shape, letter, symbol* (the distinction between letter and symbol is explained in the relevant chapter on p. 128), *word, space, sentence, text, first and beginning, last and end, middle, left, right* and *direction*. Frequent and consistent reference to these terms will help children to understand them and to use them correctly themselves.

Notices in the classroom

It is common practice in most Infant School classrooms for the teacher to label various objects and places about the room. Many teachers make considerable use of labels such as *door, window, book corner,* and so on. We recommend that this practice should be extended so that the labels are sentences rather than single words. Many teachers already do this and use the children's own language as a source for sentence labels. Rather than label the door simply *door,* have a label that reads *Jenny says the door is green but Peter says it's yellow* or *how many doors are there in our classroom?* When the children build things or make models, these can be similarly labelled with sentences: *my helicopter is rescuing Captain Scarlet* rather than *helicopter.* This is a simple extension of the writing that most teachers do when they label children's paintings.

The effect of this practice is to present words in many different contexts and this helps the children to become familiar with the words. It also strengthens the teaching of words such as *the, for, when, behind* and *of* that are not easily defined. (*Man, school, cat,* etc. can be taught with the aid of simple illustrations.)

Some of these temporary labels can be made in the teacher's stand (new words should be the same size as the teacher's words). Items brought to school by individual children and discussed in class may be put on a table with a suitable sentence in the stand. The sentence may be made by one child, a group of children or by the whole class. If the sentence contains words from the Sentence Maker, you should make reference to this and ask the group if any children know these. This is one useful way of helping the children to learn new words.

Sentences should be changed often to maintain interest in them. Few labels are read or re-read after they have been in the classroom for a couple of weeks. It is also important to draw the children's attention to the notices. Many of the children who are least conscious of written language, and who need most to be familiarised with its conventions, are the ones who overlook notices around the classroom. Re-read these examples of written language frequently so that children can learn from the repetition.

Words that refer to relationships within a family (*mum, dad, baby, auntie,* etc.) may be made into lapel cards which the children can have pinned to them when playing in the home corner.

The more the literacy work can be integrated with other activities in the classroom the better. If number, weather and colour words all match the size of the teacher's materials a great deal of work can be done with them. If you find it difficult to keep these words in their proper places you can make them on different coloured manilla – blue for number words, yellow for colour words, etc.; the children will find these easier to get out and to put away.

Arranging the materials in the classroom

It is very difficult to give specific advice about the arrangement of the work and the materials in the classroom as conditions vary so much.

There are, however, certain things that are essential to the smooth running of the scheme, once it gets under way. The Magnet Board must be at a convenient height for the children to use and should be in position right at the beginning. The teacher's Sentence Maker too needs to be ready. In schools where there is vertical grouping and sufficient room, it may be better to have the teacher's Sentence Maker and the other materials in a 'literacy corner' where the younger children will be able to work (although we would not for a moment suggest that the older children should be excluded from it). In classrooms where there is a reception class it is probably better to have the teacher's Sentence Maker more mobile, perhaps mounted on a movable stand or small clothes' horse, so that it can be put in the most convenient position at any time. If your classroom is very cramped you may have to fix the teacher's Sentence Maker to the wall or the back of a cupboard which is used to divide up the room. The important thing is that this folder must be easily seen by the children who are going to use it and it must have a surface nearby on which the teacher's stand can be rested to make sentences. You may have the teacher's Sentence Maker empty to start with and build up the vocabulary as words are used and known, or start with the words already in position. It is helpful if you have all the children's names and your own name on the blank ruled cards, so that they match the teacher's words. These are often needed in the first sentences. The blank card, with a felt-tipped pen and scissors, should be ready for when the materials start to be used, and stored near the Sentence Maker.

During the first few weeks when children are getting used to school you will have time to decide exactly where things should best be kept so that each child will know exactly where his own materials are.

Storing the Sentence Makers and Stands

The essential thing with both Sentence Makers and Stands is that they should always be stored in one place, and that the children are trained to collect and return them to this place. From the beginning children should be trained to make sure that they have returned

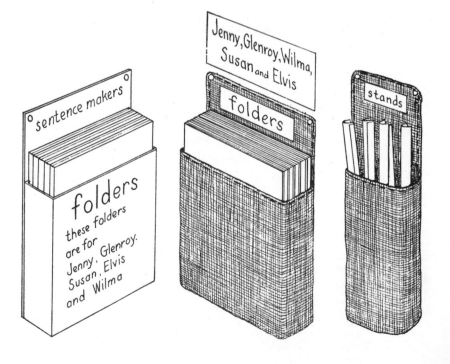

all their words to their appropriate places in the Sentence Makers.

There are several ways in which *Breakthrough* materials may be stored in the classroom. Hessian pockets could be made either for each child's Sentence Maker, or for those belonging to a group of children. (If low storage units are available in the classroom these may be used instead.) The illustrations on p. 10 show examples of pockets made of card and hessian. Each pocket has a place for listing the names of the children whose folders are stored in it (by the time children are given a Sentence Maker they are able to read their own names). The plastic Stands may be similarly stored in a pocket, or alternatively, in a box or stacked on a low shelf. The important thing is that they should be at a height easily reached by small children.

Storing the inserts

The children's word inserts are supplied in sheets with the words punched so that single words may be pressed out. If these sheets are kept together as a block, individual words can be extracted as they are needed. Or one set of words for each child may be kept between sheets of paper or broken up and the loose words kept in a box or envelope. However, this method tends to be time-consuming if the class is a large one.

Alternatively, it is possible to store words so that children can be trained eventually to find new words easily for themselves. To do this the words are best arranged in alphabetic order or in the order in which they are to be found in the Sentence Maker.

The easiest method of arranging them alphabetically is to have a store of each word in an individual envelope which has that word clearly marked on the outside. The resulting collection of envelopes may be kept in a box (index-card box, shoe box, etc.) or in a drawer. A development of this is to make a wall folder which has small pockets to hold a store of each word.

Perhaps the simplest way of arranging words in Sentence Maker order is to make a wall folder similar to

the Sentence Maker with pockets or small boxes to hold
the store of each word. An example of each is written
on the front of each small box. Alternatively, by using a
set of 'tidy' boxes, you may store a whole line of words
together, securing a bundle of each word by an elastic
band.

Learning to use written language

When a child starts work with the teacher's Sentence
Maker and later when he works with his own, he is
learning to master the complicated task of composing
written sentences without first having to master handwriting and spelling. By means of the Sentence Maker
he is responsible for converting short stretches of thinking and speaking into writing. In doing this he is given
direct experience of:

1 The left to right directionality of the English writing
   system.
2 The way in which words are separated from each other
   by word spaces.
3 The importance of the order in which words occur in
   written sentences.
4 The way that grammatical inflections such as **-ing, -s,
   -ed** are added to words.
5 Beginning the use of punctuation.
6 Learning new words in structures and not in isolation.
7 The appearance of words – through matching them
   back into place in the Sentence Maker.
8 The appearance of normal English phrases and sentences.
9 The way in which sentences may be altered by moving
   some words into new positions, and through this, learning to correct mistakes and vary sentences.
10 Reading his own sentences to himself, to other children
   and to any interested adults, thus giving him plenty of
   practice.
11 Watching you set down his sentences in his reading
   book in a way which will become a model for him.
12 Making and reading sentences which are natural to
   him and interesting because they are his own.

13 The way in which words are put together to make a sentence and the way several sentences make a story.

The experience a child gains from composing a sentence in this way is different from that of watching you write down one he has spoken. With the Sentence Maker the child learns from direct experiment to master the skills involved in using the English writing system. When you write down his spoken words he has little chance of discovering what it is that you are doing.

The use of the Magnet Board

The Magnet Board and figurines have been designed to provide a source of interest and discussion and to help the children start to use simple written language.

The figurines may be sorted out into separate groups such as outdoors, the family, story characters and they may have magnets Sellotaped to the back of them. They will also adhere to the board quite well if the magnets are just placed on top of them; the magnetism works through the thickness of the card. If you keep your magnets loose, however, bear in mind that they are very attractive to children and they may be 'borrowed'.

Various scenes both indoors and out can be set up on the board and the children can move the figurines about and describe what is happening. Your class may want to give them all names (including the witch) and develop stories about them.

The figurines may also be used to give the children practice in the use of words such as *on, in, under, through*; for example *the witch is under the table, the baby is with mum*.

We have supplied figurines to make it possible for children to set up everyday situations – family events, the arrangement of rooms, the family using everyday things, road safety – and fantasy situations. You may want to add to the stock of figurines by using suitable pictures from magazines or by using some of the children's own paintings; these should be mounted on card of a similar thickness to that supplied.

When children's spoken language is fluent and they are able to tell stories about the Magnet Board characters, words from the teacher's Sentence Maker can be used to introduce the children to written language, preferably in simple sentences, like *mum is at home with the baby.* You may wish to make additional words (for example, *policeman, kitchen*) on the teacher's blank card and these, with the words from the teacher's Sentence Maker can be attached to the Magnet Board or used in the teacher's Stand. You can also write on the Magnet Board with chalk.

The use of the teacher's Sentence Maker

The teacher's Sentence Maker is a replica of the two printed leaves of the child's. Its purpose is to introduce children to the making of sentences with printed words. The word cards are taken from the folder and slotted into the stand and when they have been used they are matched back into the Sentence Maker. Throughout the material the thick black line at the bottom of all inserts (word inserts, symbol inserts and blank inserts) is to indicate which way up they must go. In making first sentences for the children to see and discuss, it will help if you put a dot at the left hand end of the stand to show where a sentence must begin. Show the children that a word space (not more than the width of two fingers) is left between individual words and that they are placed in order from left to right.

Work with the Sentence Maker should arise from the children's own interests. In many classes a small group of children show signs of being ready to start. They will probably ask you about the Sentence Maker and the words, but if not, bring them together and ask them if they know what is on the cards. They may say letters, words, shapes, black marks; but probably someone will know that they are words. In any case make sure that the children who are starting to use the materials know that they are dealing with *words* and at all times discuss and explain what you are doing. Show them the way to make a sentence in the stand starting from the left working towards the right. Explanation and discussion will ensure that the children understand the process, especially if they put into their own words what you and they are doing.

There is only one way of using the Sentence Maker correctly and the children must learn this. There are, however, very many ways of introducing the children to it. One group began with *we are the new children*; another group who started to use the Sentence Maker the day before St Valentine's Day asked the teacher to make *I love you* so that they could put it on Valentine's cards. A good starting point may arise from work with the Magnet Board or, from words that children already know and want to use.

If you have made cards of your name and the children's names ready for this occasion you may start by saying 'I am Miss Smith'. The children count the number of words in what you have said. You then take the cards and compose *I am Miss Smith* in the stand. You read this to the children, pointing to each word as you do so. You may discuss with the children each individual word, asking them what the first word you said was, and asking them to point to the first word you put in the stand. You then do the same thing with the other words. Next you ask one of the children to read the sentence while you point to the words. When the child has done this and read 'I am Miss Smith' you ask 'Are you Miss Smith?' The child replies 'No, I am Charlie'. You show him the card with *Charlie* written on it and ask him if he can alter the sentence to *I am Charlie*. He will almost certainly need help in doing this at first. Each child in the group then alters the sentence appropriately and reads it aloud to the group, pointing to the words as they are read. The sentences made in this first lesson may be written out on a sheet of paper and pinned to the wall, where the group may return during the day and re-read the sentences and re-make them if they want to.

The next lesson may consist of altering *I am a teacher* to *I am a boy* or *I am a girl*. The procedure will be similar to that of the first lesson. This work must be done in very small groups and should be informal and relaxed. Putting the words away in the teacher's Sentence

Maker and changing the words in the stand should be regarded as a kind of game.

This work can be extended quite soon with the faster children, as you introduce new words and sentence forms such as questions and commands. The children should soon learn to alter the sentence by themselves, and should be encouraged to suggest starting points for the group lessons.

The sentence work will gradually develop, with more and more children joining in. The first group may soon divide up with some children working quite slowly and others racing ahead. As more children begin on this work, the groups will be at different stages, and the teacher must change the groups around frequently to cope with the different rates of development and interest. At first the children will make lots of mistakes and will put words in the wrong place or leave words out altogether. This is quite normal and the children should not be subjected to constant correction. Most of the children can be led to discover their own mistakes. If, for example, a child leaves out a word or puts one in the wrong place, it is usually enough to ask him to read the sentence aloud, pointing to each word as he reads it. This will, in fact, show whether or not he understands what he is reading, or is just memorising.

Word order is very important in English. *George loves Jane* means something quite different from *Jane loves George*. Children find this very difficult to grasp in written language and will often jumble the words. Sometimes they will write *mum home* and read it as *my mum is at home*, but drawing the child's attention to the number of words in the spoken sentence, comparing it with the written sentence, and having the child read it slowly and carefully will help sort out the mistake. Do not insist too strongly on the child finding the mistake. Some children may consistently make the same type of error for several weeks before understanding why it is wrong and how to correct it.

The training children are given on the teacher's Sentence Maker is essential to the successful use of the individual Sentence Makers and the children should not be hurried over this stage. For a child to recognise a word does not mean that he *knows* it; he must be able to match it back into its correct place in the Sentence Maker; he must be able to use it to compose a sentence and he must be able to read it with confidence in different contexts.

When a child knows, in this sense, about 12 of the words, you may consider him to be ready to start using his own Sentence Maker.

The *best* method of introducing work with the Sentence Maker is for the teacher to use a starting sentence derived from something in which the group, or an individual, is most keenly interested.

2

THE CHILDREN'S SENTENCE MAKER

The Sentence Maker is the heart of the literacy work. In using this piece of equipment the responsibility for ordering written English for the first time falls upon the child and, at the same time, he is composing his first reading book. Under 'Learning to use written language', page 12, we have listed the important points learned in the course of using the Sentence Maker.

We have suggested that the point at which a child really knows 12 words may be the best time for him to start using his own Sentence Maker, but the exact point for starting any child must be decided by you; it may be that a very slow child will be greatly encouraged by having a Sentence Maker although he can only operate with five or six words, but another child may come into school already knowing a number of words and very soon be able to use them. When the child gets his own Sentence Maker it contains only the words which he knows and his own name written on card in the space for personal words (the right-hand leaf).

When a child starts to work independently he should know:

1 Exactly where to get his Sentence Maker and Stand and that he must put it back with the inserts in their proper place.

2 That he will need a clear space on a table top on which to stand his folder, with the Stand in front of it.

3 Where he can get new words, printed or personal. You may wish to sit centrally at certain times ready to give out new words or you may let children come and ask for them as soon as they want them. Whatever you decide to do make sure that the child knows the procedure.

4 That sentence making and reading is a social activity

and that he can share sentences with his neighbours; children gain a great deal of knowledge and interest from reading each other's sentences.

5 Whether you want him to take his sentences to you to be written in his sentence book or whether you will come to him. If you are too busy at the time a sentence has been made, you may ask children to put their name cards at the end of the sentences they have composed and leave them in a pre-arranged place for you to write out later.

It is very important that the children's reading of their sentences should not be neglected. Some of these will be put up round the room (see 'Using the children's sentences', page 29) and later, some children will attempt to write out their sentences for themselves. Despite this, *it is very important that each child has his own book in which you write the sentences he has composed, clearly and neatly.* Only in this way can the child have a perfect record of his work. If the date is entered at regular intervals you will be able to check the amount of work being done and assess the progress made in a given period.

An early entry in a child's sentence book might read:
   I am a boy.
A later entry in the same book:
   I was late to school because I fell over
and still later, in a second or third book there might be:
   I told my mum not to let the baby go out for walks in the road because she might get run over and have to go to hospital or die.

At first some children like to illustrate the sentence you have copied into their books. Later they may not wish to do so because the composing of sentences is sufficiently satisfying in itself. It is these sentences that make up the child's first reading books.

Although children learn a great deal from reading other children's sentences, from sentences written under their paintings and on the Magnet Board, it has never been our intention that they should use the Sentence Makers to copy other people's sentences. *This book of sentences should include only those sentences composed by the child himself.*

If a child repeatedly makes one particular sentence over a period, it may indicate that he has been given his own Sentence Maker a little too soon or that he is unsure of how to go on. It may be necessary to bring him into a group which is still working with the teacher's Sentence Maker and to give him more confidence through guided practice.

The wide variety of sentences which children compose with *Breakthrough* material contrast vividly with the sentences found in traditional first reading books. Early sentences may show the practice element which is very evident in the first sentences of babies learning to speak. A child may make sentences like:

I am big.
my teacher is big.
my mum is big.
my dad is big.
my baby is little.
my book is little.
my friend is little.

Children will take great pleasure in this kind of practice and shortly afterwards will experiment with new kinds of sentences.

The following sentences are examples of the way in which children demonstrate the variety of their practice and experiment. The first two groups of sentences show how two children altered original sentences. The last group shows the way in which local and national events were incorporated into their work. Sentence length at this stage is varied.

I am happy. I am big. I am a big girl. Are you? I love you. I love my mum. My mum is at home. I like my mum. I like my teacher.

My sister is at school. Do you like school? Do you like me? Yes. I'm doing my sentences. I'm not doing sentences today. Watch me do sentences. My television is watching me.

Concorde can fly. Miss Smith is in the bath. I was out last night. We made some flags to wave on the dark mornings. My mum went to the hairdressers last night and my dad said she looked beautiful. My dad kissed my mum. Princess Anne launched the Esso Northumbria.

Getting new words for the Sentence Maker

Each child will have a number of words in his folder that few other children have. When a group of children work together, showing each other their sentences, they have the opportunity to see and read new words. New words will also be learned from notices round the room and from the children's sentences which have been written on sheets or in wall books.

It is possible that you may want to teach new words for a special purpose. You may wish to take a group for work with words associated with a centre of activity or some immediate interest. If, for example, the class has just returned from a particularly enjoyable music and movement lesson, you may wish to teach the written form of some of the associated action words. You might construct *the children run* and then alter the final word to *skip, play, jump* or *walk*. The children may be allowed to act out the movement or you may make commands in the teacher's stand such as *Charlie jump to your friend*; *skip around the room Mary* or *walk to the table*. You might like to encourage the children to make instructions such as *go to the door teacher*. You should not feel that teaching new words in a direct manner is undesirable.

Sometimes you may want to prepare a sentence in the Stand before the children come into the room; for example *can you see the flowers I have put on my table?* and await results. If this appears regularly it will develop into a game so that the children will always look for new sentences around the room. Alternatively, *when I get up* can be put into the Stand so that the children have to complete it with the words they already know.

All these exercises in written language should be linked to the printed vocabulary of the Sentence Maker whenever possible. Some teachers have made class diaries where they enter sentences that are made after general discussion. This diary may be a large book in which sheets can be pasted, or simply several sheets of paper clipped to an easel. This kind of activity is very useful for revising aspects of the writing system learnt in the earlier stages of the programme, such as directionality, word spacing, the meaning of word, letter, space, etc. If the diary entry is, for example, *Peter has a new baby sister*, the teacher may ask the children to find *has*, *a* and *baby* from the teacher's Sentence Maker. The most useful feature of this kind of activity is not only that it connects the work of the class to a central organised course, but that it helps the children to learn words such as *has*, *for*, *the*, etc., by presenting them in many different contexts.

Personal words

The right-hand leaf of the Sentence Maker is blank. This is a store for the personal words which children will need. The printed vocabulary is common to them all and the words it contains should be acquired steadily, without the personal store ever becoming swamped by too many new words.

The first personal words that a child will ask for will be about himself. He will have his own name when he gets his own Sentence Maker but he will probably want the names of his family and friends. The blank cards, which are the inserts for the personal words, are lightly ruled so that words written on them by the teacher will be at the same level as the printed words when placed in the stand. Children use a variety of different words to refer to their parents. We have printed the most popular – *mum* and *dad* – and space has been left so that these may be changed to *mummy* and *daddy*. It is easy to change *mum* to *mom* or *mam* if either is the form children use.

It is unlikely that many of the words in the personal collection will be shared by more than a few children. However, if you find that most of the children in the class are asking for words which do not appear in the printed vocabulary this is probably a sign that you should make an extra store of these words.

The personal words a child accumulates will depend on his interests. He may have a collection like: *Andrew, Mary, gran, fish, chips, Captain Scarlet, scare, Dr Who, hospital, nurse, Saturday, ray gun, snow, football, Concorde.*
The provision of words connected with some popular

theme, stored in a box or an extra folder will help to prevent the overloading of the personal word leaf. Children can then use these words when they need them and return them to the box or folder afterwards. At Christmas or at the time of some very popular television serial a vocabulary of special words will be needed by a number of children. If you can make these in advance and arrange them so that they are accessible to the children, each child will not then need a set of words for himself. Words to do with class outings or projects can be prepared in the same way. Each child should accumulate words in his Sentence Maker at a speed which does not place any strain on his ability to recognise these readily. *The purpose of using the Sentence Maker is not only to acquire more and more words on sight recognition but also to explore the use of words and their combination in grammatical patterns.* A balance between the printed vocabulary and the personal words must be kept. While the printed vocabulary is in no way a set list which must be learned first, nevertheless normal English sentence patterns need most of these words.

When a large number of personal words are used only occasionally are they likely to be forgotten. The Sentence Maker should contain a store of words which can be recognised with ease and used with confidence. It may be necessary for you to check that children have not acquired words in which they have, for the moment, lost interest and for you to remove these when this is the case. *It is the constant use of words to compose a variety of texts that ensures that the child will remember them.*

At a later stage when children have become familiar with the Word Maker they will often spell a new word into their sentences rather than ask you to make it for them on blank card.

Some stages in learning to operate the Sentence Maker

The stages we have set out below mark a progression towards an ability to make sentences, but all children will not pass through all the stages in the order indicated. We have set them out primarily to show what the child may be considered to have achieved at each stage, not to show how much he is falling below a standard in written English. Some children will move fairly slowly from one stage to the next, while others will learn quite quickly and then, maybe weeks or months later, slip back into making mistakes associated with an earlier stage; do not worry about this or let the child feel that he has failed in any way; it happens very often and is quite normal.

One of the advantages of using the Sentence Maker is that it enables the teacher to see how much the child has learned; each stage that the child masters is an achievement that can and should be praised by the teacher. However, the stages will never be evidenced if the child deals only with static written language in reading texts and in copying from the teacher's handwriting. In addition, the Sentence Maker and stand enable the child to alter his written language easily, add to it, correct any mistakes he may notice and discuss his work with the teacher in a way quite impossible in other circumstances.

1 Listing words

Since the initial reading vocabulary has been learnt as 'look and say' it is hardly surprising that many children simply place the words they know in the Stand and read them back as separate items with no grammatical links at all. *Mum dad is home Glenroy* is an example of this listing. But you may notice that the child has learned to associate the marks on the cards with the noises he makes with his mouth, that he has discovered the possibility of using words as separate units and that he may be reading the list from left to right, showing an awareness of the directionality of the writing system.

2 Sentences with words left out

For many children the next stage is to produce sentences from which certain words have been omitted. *Baby little* may be read back as *the baby is little*. The words which give the grammatical structure to the sentence are added by the child as he reads. This is an obvious advance over the earlier stage: they are now producing 'telegram' sentences. Later the words which they have regarded as less important may be added at the end – *mum home my is at*. This is an interesting stage; do not be too concerned with making the child produce a complete sentence. Get him to read what he has done and point to each word as he reads it. In this way he will often stop and correct his sentence when he sees what has happened; if he doesn't, let him add to or change the sentence as he reads it, without insisting that the written word order be changed. Praise the child for reading from left to right and discuss the meaning of his sentence with him. These early examples should not be written in the child's book – he will soon be writing grammatical sentences. When *this* happens start to keep a record of work for him to read.

3 Making partial sentences

A child may start by making what we usually regard as parts of sentences; they may be just groups of words such as *boy and girl and little baby* or *my big teacher*; this may be the result of working with the Magnet Board and labelling the figurines. This is perfectly acceptable and these examples should be written in the child's book and illustrated. Some of our first reading books, *big and little*, for example, include phrases of this type. The additional learning evidenced by this is that of ordering words within a group – the language permits us to make *three pretty little girls* and not *little pretty three girls*. Children are likely to notice the rules which order the words in a noun phrase for the first time when they try to represent them in written language (they will seldom make a mistake in their speech).

4 Deviant sentence forms

Sometimes the children may set up a noun and then say something about it, for example *my little teacher I love*; this should be accepted without correction, it is not likely to become an established practice. If it persists, deal with some examples of it with a small group and discuss alternatives with them.

5 Inflections

When the children begin to use inflectional endings in
the Folder (**es, ed, ing, s**) common spelling faults such
as *runing, geting, takeing, crys,* will be made. This is
discussed in the section on spelling; at this stage it is
not profitable to insist on the correct spelling of in-
flected forms. Accept what the child has put for the
time being, only point out that if the sentence is copied
into the child's special book you have put *running* instead of *runing.* If an individual or a small group of
children repeatedly make a mistake of this type it may
be time to take a lesson on one of these inflectional
changes. With many children the incorrect form will
be discarded as he moves on and this stage is comparable with much younger children using spoken
forms such as *goed, amn't, be-ed.*

The main point about the 'mistakes' that occur when
a child is learning to use the Sentence Maker is that
they give insight into the way in which the child is
learning, and indicate what further information he
needs. Always note what the child has got right, as
well as the errors he has made and praise him for the
progress he is making. Certain types of error are discussed in greater detail in Part Two (see page 99).

What to do when the Sentence Maker is complete

By the time a child has filled his Sentence Maker he will
have come to rely on it less and less for help in producing written sentences. You will notice him writing
sentences and stories without using the Stand. By this
time he will also have a stock of his own words in the
blank section of the Folder.

Make sure that the child has been using the Folder to
show his ability to cope with different aspects of written
work; that he is able to use all the affixes **-ed, -ing,
-es, -s;** that he is able to extend and alter his sentences
by adding adjectives, phrases and clauses in the correct
place and that he feels very confident about handling
written language within the limits of his present knowledge.

There is an opportunity now to help the child internalise some of the spelling patterns of English. He should, by this stage, be used to working out some spelling patterns (see the use of the Word Maker, page 30) and he can now be asked to arrange the words in a variety of patterns, making lists of words such as *boy, book, bird, bed, big, bad, by, be* (as will be explained later). He can also make lists of words with common symbols – street, see, sleep, tree, been by taking out the words and arranging them in sets on his table. Lists of this type can be written into a class spelling book, on a wall chart, or individuals can make their own lists in books. (See also the suggestions under 'Stages in the use of the Word Maker', page 105.) The final use to which the words from the Sentence Maker may be put is for the child to arrange them all for his first dictionary. Provide him with a book in which the pages have been headed by initial symbols in alphabetical order – **a, b, c, ch**, etc. When the child has arranged his words in order by the initial symbol, check them and let him write them in his book. Other words may be added later and this is a good opportunity to show children dictionaries and telephone directories, so that they may see the reason for arranging items in this way, and learn how to find what they are looking for. At this time too he can learn to look up items in *An abc for hungry girls and boys* and in *About the house.*

The advantages of producing a dictionary in this way are:

1 The child knows the initial entries very well. Under 'b' for example, he will see words which he has used for some time, such as *be, big, boy*, etc., and he will be able to relate the shape and sound representation of the initial symbol to these in new words such as *black, bring.*

2 The child himself has been led to discover the way the alphabetical arrangement of symbols works, instead of having an inexplicable, arbitrary ordering imposed on him.

3 The organisation presents symbols (and therefore includes **c** as in **c**at, **c** as in **c**ity, **ch** as in **ch**urch, **s** as in **s**it, **sh** as in **sh**ip) rather than letters so as to help him to sort out the way symbols represent sounds.

In schools with vertical streaming, where children who are already reading and writing quite well see the younger ones starting with the *Breakthrough* materials, teachers have begun to notice a marked improvement in their writing. This is probably due to the fact that they go to the literacy corner and experiment with sentences themselves, discussing these experiments with each other, with younger children and with the teacher; all the time they are building up a wider knowledge of English in action. For this reason, and because we do not ever want a child to feel that some important part of the learning process is 'complete' and must be discontinued, do not be too hasty in encouraging any child to put away his Sentence Maker for good. He may still like to try things out. He may revert to using the words and the stand for a time after he has shown that he can write without them and you may want to show him how he could vary his sentences to make them more interesting. In time the Sentence Maker will be dispensed with naturally. Nothing is to be gained by hastening the process or by making the child feel that it is a backward step to want to use it again.

Reusing the Sentence Maker

The children's Sentence Maker consists of the triptych folder, the sheets of printed inserts to fill the two printed leaves and blanks for the unprinted personal leaf of the folder. The folder itself should last for several years, the inserts may have to be replaced as the folder is passed on.

There must be no pressure on children to discard their folders. Some children may need the help of the folder for some time and there may well be those who need to take it with them into the Junior School, thus ensuring continuity of progress at what is for many children a critical stage in their literacy learning. When a child, or a group of children, has entered all the words from the Sentence Makers into word books or dictionaries and after they have played many of the word games outlined here, and when they no longer need to refer to their folders frequently to check spellings, the folders may be taken from the children and given to the beginners in the reception class.

The children who have completed work with the folders may find it useful to have a single copy of the Sentence Maker in the classroom which they may use for reference purposes such as the working out of new spellings (working out *fight* by referring to the spelling pattern represented in the folder by *night* for example) playing word games involving the manipulation of the insert cards, trying out possible grammatical constructions or learning the use of unfamiliar punctuation marks.

If, when the Sentence Makers are passed down to the lower class, the personal word leaf has not been written on or written on only in pencil, this will make the revise of the materials simpler. The punchout sheets of printed inserts are available separately. These will most probably need replacing. If the inserts have been kept well it may only be necessary to write out a few words such as the much-used *I* and *my* on the blank cards and use the inserts over again also.

Using the children's sentences

The primary use of a child's sentences is to make his first reading book; but the greater the sharing of interest in sentences, the more reading material there is available. This sharing may take place directly between neighbours who read each other's sentences or when a selection of interesting sentences is written on a large sheet entitled 'Sentences we have made'. Later on when the children start to write stories there can be a wall book of 'Stories we have written'.

With a little encouragement, children will think of many ways of using their sentences. They can leave a sentence in a stand in front of a model they have made or under a picture they have painted. The children may put their sentences together to make books of different sizes, and on many different topics. One child may be able to make one book, or at least supply the text for it, or you may take sentences on the same topic from several children and make a book from these.

3

INTRODUCING AND USING THE WORD MAKER

You may find it useful to make a large version of the Word Maker to use with groups of children in the same way that you have used the Sentence Maker. There is certainly an advantage in starting on a large model before the child transfers to the small one.. On the other hand we would not suggest that the child is introduced to the Word Maker in any form until he has become quite proficient with the Sentence Maker.

Rather than talk about 'letters' when using the Word Makers try to use the term *symbol* and teach it to the children. Much confusion arises from the belief that there is a simple and direct relationship between single letters and sounds. This may be true in some cases (although it is arguable even in what may seem to be obvious instances) but it is basically a mistaken idea. The word *shop* for example is made up of three symbols **sh**, **o** and **p**, but from four letters **s**, **h**, **o** and **p**. It is a great help if the children can acquire from the beginning the vocabulary they need for talking and thinking about words and spelling. The term *letter* should be used only when referring to the single items we use in writing words, as in handwriting instruction, while *symbol* is a term to use when dealing with spelling.

The reason for starting the use of the Word Maker may arise because a child has put a word back in the Sentence Maker in the wrong place. He may put *and* back where *dad* should be, or *on* back where *no* should be. This is an opportunity for him to look at the structure of words more closely, to see that symbols must follow each other from left to right (as words do in a sentence), and to learn to look more closely at the individual letter shapes.

When a child has quite a large number of words in his Sentence Maker and has been composing sentences well, his attention should be directed to the internal structure of words. One of the best times to start using the Word Maker may be when a child asks for a new personal word which has a simple sound/symbol correspondence; suppose he asks for 'best'. Say to him 'What do you think it begins with?' if he says 'b' (naming the letter) or 'That one' (picking the letter out) ask him to try and make the word. Quite soon a child will start to spell the word in a Word Maker before coming to ask if it is correct, and later still he may spell the word straight into a sentence on the stand, using the symbol cards from the Word Maker in place of a hand-written word.

When the child begins to learn sound/symbol correspondences, lists of words such as *bad, dad, sad, had* and *mad* can be constructed in a pocket of the Word Maker, and compared. The alteration of the initial symbol is the simplest way to begin to teach the child how to make strings of words with related spelling patterns. After a while the procedure can be varied by changing the final and then middle symbol as well. A great deal of practice is needed, with children working in groups or with you, before they learn to do this confidently. The practice may be in the form of games or of specific teaching, and the same ground must be covered often to reinforce this first stage in the learning of spelling patterns. When the child has had a considerable amount of practice in changing the initial symbols, he can be encouraged to try changing final symbols (as in *had, has, hat, ham*), and later still the medial symbol (as in *has, his; bad, bed*). The latter are rather difficult for some children, and you should proceed slowly. The children should never feel under pressure nor be allowed to become discouraged.

All the children, either separately or in groups, should be encouraged to build up lists of words as a result of changing symbols:

Changing initial symbol	Changing final symbol	Changing middle symbol
in	can	bed
bin	cap	bad
chin	cab	bid
din	cat	bud
pin		
spin		
tin		
thin		
win		

It does not matter if the children produce possible words which have not yet appeared in the English language, for example, *hin*, *cag*, *bod*. These are acceptable English spellings, unlike *nhi*, *gca* or *obd*. Making words like these will also serve to consolidate ideas about the spelling patterns. The children could invent possible meanings for any new words they may make up.

Eventually children should also be able to change *any* symbol in a word to make it into another word. This is a later development of the ability to make lists by changing the symbol in one position in the word. It may result in a list of words like *tap*, *rap*, *rat*, *hat*, *hot*, etc. Words in which final consonants are doubled can be dealt with separately (e.g. *hill*, *mill*, *miss*, etc.), but only the most advanced children would be able to show any interest in this during the first stage of the literacy programme. These games may be played often but do not allow them to become too complicated. The simpler words will produce more alternatives and will make the point at issue clearer.

When the children are using the Word Makers teach them to look for the symbols systematically along the lines from the top left hand corner to the bottom of the right-hand leaf. Later they may notice that the consonants and vowels are stored separately in the left and right hand leaves of the Word Maker. The children may come to realise that, for example, the vowels occupy the middle place in simple single syllable words such as *can*, *had*, *sit*, etc.

If each child does not have his own Word Maker, they

should be kept centrally where the children can get one when they need it.

The spelling of words in the Word Maker or in a Stand, symbol by symbol, gives a child plenty of opportunity to experiment and perfect a spelling pattern. It also gives you the opportunity to discuss various spelling patterns, pointing out regularities and exceptions. Alterations can be more clearly and easily made in this folder than when a child has to rewrite or rub out symbols written in a book.

The Word Makers are an integral part of the literacy work. They are intended to reinforce the work in the Sentence Makers and to help the child recognise words accurately and make some attempt to read and write words he has not met before.

The place of spelling in learning to read and write

Some infant teachers will feel that there is no place for this subject in the Infants' classroom and it is often left entirely to the Junior School to teach spelling. Teachers in the upper Junior School or those taking remedial classes in Secondary Schools often feel that the teaching of spelling has been left too late and that once children establish an incorrect spelling form it is very difficult to change it. We do not suggest that small children become so spelling conscious that they are hindered from writing freely, but we do believe that a painless beginning can be made in the Infants' School which will be very helpful to all children.

There are specific aids to word recognition and spelling built into the *Breakthrough* materials.

1 The children have whole words before them from the beginning of the literacy programme. They are matching these words from the start and later copying them into books and on paper. By the time they begin writing without the aid of the Sentence Maker many spelling patterns will have been established.

2 The children's attention is specifically drawn to the structure of words. They compare words and look closely at those which are confusing or difficult to remember by using the Word Maker.

3 The aim of the spelling games is to draw attention to the way in which symbols combine to make words.

4 The emphasis placed on symbols rather than letters in the Word Maker makes it easier for the children to work out spellings for themselves.

It would be much simpler if it were possible to approach the relationship between sound and symbol as invariate. But the complexity of English spelling and the number of regional dialects and local accents account for the great variety in these relationships; the word 'come' may sound quite different when spoken in the South of England, the North of England or by a West Indian. The vowels of English present most variation and difficulty; the consonants are more easily dealt with. When you are drawing attention to single sounds or to the pronunciation of words, remember that the children's sounds may not correspond to symbols in the same way as yours. It is difficult for you to be fully aware of all the sounds to be found in children's speech (in some classes several markedly different accents may be represented). Children therefore need help to relate *their own speech sounds to the written symbols*.

Despite the complexity of English spelling, there are many regular spelling patterns. These are dealt with in some detail in Appendix I, p. 164. The following points are relevant to the early stages of learning to read and write:

1 The structure of written syllables can be explored by means of the Word Maker. Word games help to establish knowledge of symbols and the way they represent speech sounds, and to encourage children to discover how words are made. However, knowing how to spell, remembering the words which belong to a certain spelling pattern will come more easily if the words are used in composing sentences.

2 The idea that a symbol may *represent a sound* or may. be used as a marker to show some other spelling feature, can be introduced quite easily. We suggest the use of the term 'marker' in preference to a description such as 'the magic e' because the word 'marker' is meaningful and the other is not. The most common example of the final **e** marker is found in words like

mate, fine, hope. Without the **e** marker we write *mat, fin, hop.*

3 If a group of children are specially interested in this work, you may go on to show how the addition of **-ing** to words eliminates the final **e** in words and doubles the final consonant in words with short vowels. For example: *hop – hopping,* but *hope – hoping; mat – matting,* but *mate – mating; rid – ridding,* but *ride – riding.*

4 The regular formation of plurals by the addition of **s**, except after the symbols **s**, **sh**, **ch**, and **x** (where **es** must be added), and the addition of **-ed** to certain verbs can be demonstrated.

5 At all times the children should be encouraged to try to spell new words for themselves. After they have done so you should try to understand how any mistake in doing this has arisen. (e.g., *mist* for *missed,* where the child has noted the sound of the word without understanding the relationship of the word *missed* to the verb *to miss*). When the children encounter new words in the course of their reading encourage them to try and understand these in terms of sound/symbol correspondences. When they need new words while writing, they should be encouraged to attempt to work them out for themselves in the Word Maker rather than to appeal to the teacher for the correct spelling or to guess in a random fashion. The build-up of the knowledge of spelling patterns is, at this stage, likely to be slow, but it is of great importance.

6 If the faster children repeatedly mis-spell a common word, then this should be corrected and discussed with the individuals concerned. We hope that few of these mistakes will occur, and, that when they do, it will be easier to help the child to understand where he has made his mistake, because he has some knowledge of the structure of words and some practice in dealing with symbols.

Spelling games

One of the most useful games has proved to be that in which one symbol of a word is taken out and another substituted to make a different word.

Others which the children have enjoyed have been:
1 A child takes the symbols to spell his own name and then makes as many words as he can from these symbols.
2 The children discover how many words with a similar spelling pattern they can collect from their Sentence Maker, from writing around the room and from books. For example words beginning with the consonant symbol **sh**. At another time they can collect words beginning with symbol **s** or symbol **h**.
3 If you have the teacher's version of the Word Maker, give four children one symbol each from a word you have chosen and get them to arrange themselves as that word (this game can also be played with words to make a simple sentence). Unscrambling symbols can also be played by two children with the small Word Maker.
4 A small group of children sit round a table. One is the caller and he has several simple pictures with the name of the object written on the back: for example *cat*, *tree*, etc. The other children in the group try to spell the word on the Word Maker and the first one correct becomes caller.
5 Read out a very short list of words with the same initial symbol and get the children to hold up this symbol as soon as they recognise it.

Punctuation

It may seem strange to many Infants' teachers to have to deal with punctuation in the first part of the literacy programme. It is a subject which is often left until much later. You will find the full stop and the question mark in the Sentence Maker. The use of these punctuation marks can be discussed very soon after children start to make sentences freely for themselves. They may enquire about the marks themselves, or discussion about them may arise from your teaching. In encouraging children to read in a natural voice, you may point out that the question mark is used in writing to replace the questioning intonation in speech. When children start to write more than one sentence, or before, if they show interest, the full stop can be introduced as a mark to show that one sentence is complete. Use these two marks in work on the teacher's Stand with children who are already able to make sentences quite well, but not with beginners.

Note: in *Breakthrough* books we have used only these first punctuation marks and in the slightly harder ones capital letters at the beginning of sentences.

Capital letters

When children are able to work very easily with their Sentence Makers or when they need them only for reference, you may want to show them how to begin their sentences with capital letters. For this they have to learn some new letter shapes and some that are merely larger versions of the ones they already know. They can check on these differences (as well as on the printer's *a* and *g*) by looking at the alphabet printed on the cover of the Sentence Maker. If handwritten sets of capitals are ready in a small box, advanced children may substitute them for the lower case letters at the beginning of sentences. The children will already be familiar with capital I and with the capital in their names. They can also be shown how picture story books make use of capitals.

A note on class teaching

The use of the *Breakthrough* materials in the classroom is open to considerable personal interpretation; we have tried to incorporate in this manual as many ideas as possible, but you will be able to think of many other ways of using the materials, sometimes with individuals, sometimes with a group and sometimes with the whole class. We have thought of the materials as being used by individuals and by small groups, but this does not exclude class work at times, and it may sometimes be convenient or essential for the teacher to take the whole class for some of the literacy work. The term 'class teaching' applied to the Infants' School calls forth in some teachers an immediate emotional response; it conjures up a return to seated rows of children, to rote learning and continuous instruction by the teacher – the Victorian classroom of the most repressive type. If there were no choice between repression of this type and complete freedom, then freedom in the Infant classroom should undoubtedly triumph; but there is an honourable compromise. Infants' teachers speak to their class as a whole at different times of the day, and the children are usually all together for story telling and reading. *You will not be failing or harming the children if you take teaching points in the same way, as long as you give groups or individuals attention at another time.*

4

BOOKS IN THE CLASSROOM

Children should have access to as many good children's books as possible to encourage them to develop an interest in and an attachment to books and to give them the desire to read for themselves. Books specially recommended for use in various ways are included in the Appendices. Others could have been added but these lists are intended only as a guide. The books to be found there have been chosen particularly with a view to introducing children to children's literature from the beginning rather than to 'reading books', which are seen as being different and separate from children's literature. Children should not feel that any of the books in the classroom are to be 'got through' as fast as possible or that they are only the means to an end.

Books made in the classroom

These include books made by the teacher, by the class together, by a group or by an individual child.

Teachers know very well the way in which interest springs spontaneously from incidents in the class, birthdays, special weather conditions, a fire, the opening of a new block of flats, the demolition of some houses, etc., and from special outings. Children usually have plenty of opportunity to discuss these events, but if they can sometimes be encouraged to write what they can about them afterwards, very good books of immediate interest can be made. They should be encouraged to show these to visitors and to read them to each other, not forgetting too soon the earliest books made.

Books of this kind do not always need to be factual;

imaginative ones can be made too. The important thing is that children's writing should also be part of all that they read. The books should be as attractive and as strong as possible, and in a variety of sizes from wall books to very small books. The pages can be made of white paper which is then mounted on coloured pages, or of sugar paper. A very attractive wall book of short stories can be made on a small set of hinged arms (as in a clothes' airer) with a story on large paper hanging down from each arm; or the stories can be mounted on a continuous scroll of paper.

Later, when some children are writing fairly freely they should be encouraged to write in as many different forms as possible – stories, letters, rhymes, poems, instructions. Rather than have all this writing locked away in individual books, as much of it as possible should be available to the other children to read – unless it is the wish of a child that some writing should be private. Books of instructions on how to make or how to do something can be made by the children, daily news items can be made into a newspaper, letters (and their replies) can be set out, descriptions of people or things can be put up so that others have to guess whom or what these describe.

Breakthrough books

In traditional literacy teaching children would be introduced early to special reading books. *Breakthrough* aims to give children a good deal of experience in composing natural English sentences and of reading them in books made in the classroom, before they are expected to read printed books.

This is not to suggest that some of the *Breakthrough* books should not be put in the book corner with the picture story books and from time to time read to the children and discussed. We would like them to be used in the first place exactly as the picture story books are used. You will find, however, that if you do not ask the children to start reading them too soon, the experience they have gained from using their Sentence Makers will enable them to read most *Breakthrough* books easily and with enjoyment. Because we have not intended these books to be a series through which each child must progress vertically, and because of the great variety of written sentences the children will have read before they come to printed books, it has not been necessary to grade the books in the traditional manner. There is no attempt to repeat certain words frequently; we have been more concerned that the grammatical construction of the sentences should be similar to those of normal speech and to the children's own composed sentences.

We hope that the children will find all the books interesting. In writing them we had several different purposes in mind and we hope that they will become more than a bridge between the child's own sentence book and the world of printed books generally. We have been fortunate in having illustrators who have provided a great deal of visual detail to offer talking points for children.

Apart from these general points about their use, we had certain specific purposes in mind when we wrote the *Breakthrough* books:

1 Some of the books are based upon situations common to all small children of Infant School age. Children should be able to identify or compare themselves with the child in *The loose tooth,* or to discuss their opinions about the home and school in books such as *Dressing up* or *my mum.*

2 Some books show experiences and backgrounds which may not be familiar to your children; most children will not have been *The lost girl* and rural children may not shop in the supermarket setting of *Shopping.* But here we hope that the novelty of place or situation will help talk to develop.

3 *People in stories* and *My story* have been designed to introduce traditional story book characters to children who may not be too familiar with them when they come to school. On the other hand we hope that the illustrations will make these books interesting to children who are already familiar with giants, witches and other exotic characters.

4 Books such as *a fish book* and *Birds* are intended to be used as information books. We hope that teacher and

children will make many more like them on many other subjects.

5 *a cup of tea* is a book about how to do something step by step. Here again we hope it will encourage similar books to develop in the classroom – on as many topics as possible, such as *a doll's dress, a model boat* and so on.

The colour code distinguishes the 12 easier books (which have no capital letters at the beginning of sentences) from the 12 that are somewhat more difficult (and which include the use of capitals). We do not believe that children need to know these additional letter shapes at first, but soon they must be introduced to them and their purpose discussed, because it is not long before they will meet them in other books and need them in their own writing.

The two books, *An abc for hungry girls and boys* and *About the house* are intended to be used as simple reference books in which children can look things up for themselves. Both books provide information to help children with their writing. They are also intended to encourage discussion and to be models on which similar information books could be made in the class.

Picture story books

The book corner should include books that are varied in shape and size, varied in style (of writing and of illustration), of different grades of difficulty and varied in subject matter. The books should be used for story times. They should be discussed and illustrations compared. Later on, when the children start to write, they should be encouraged to write what they think about some of the books in the corner, and this can be put up for the other children to read. Whether they agree or disagree can become the basis for discussion.

Early in the school year you should introduce the children to the book corner. Show them some of the individual books and how they are to be kept on the shelves or book stand, explaining that they must be replaced after use. Show them the correct way of opening a new book for the first time (placing it on a flat surface on its spine and opening back the covers first, then the pages in groups so that the binding will not break). As the children learn from your example to handle books with care, it is not necessary to confine their use to the book corner; you may want to have a special project display and children may want to take a book away to their own table. However, the corner should be quiet and orderly.

Some of the books in the corner may have been bought for the classroom. This supply is likely to be comparatively small as books of good quality are expensive. However, these can be augmented by books borrowed from education libraries and public libraries. Most education authorities have made some arrangements about borrowing books for this purpose. The use of loan schemes gives the children a chance to see a very wide range of books and offers them a greater opportunity to develop their ability to choose books carefully and to establish favourites (which may later be bought for the classroom library).

However the books have been acquired, at least once a term remove them all and see that they are in good condition; you may like to have the books divided into two sets which are changed over on this occasion; but the children should see that the state of the books really matters and they should feel that it is their responsibility to care for them and keep the corner tidy.

The practice of reading stories to children at least once a day is common in most Infant Schools, and this is a very valuable time. It is not, as it may sometimes appear, a time of relaxation only; it is an important teaching and learning time, for listening is not a passive skill. On the contrary, it requires great concentration on the part of the listener. When they are listening to stories, children are learning the intonation patterns of spoken English, the grammatical patterns, styles of writing, the way in which the main story can be carried through minor incidents and conversations, factual information about the world and other people and, more obviously, an extension of vocabulary. Even a book which may seem too difficult for most of the class may prove to be extremely popular; the more receptive children will learn much from it and even the slower ones will be absorbing a great deal of new information. The greater the variety, in style and subject matter, of books read to the class, the wider the field of learning; but children should also be able to establish their favourites, which may be read and re-read.

The time of reading and discussing books should also include introduction to and discussion of the use of the public libraries. Many of the books used at this time will be library books, and the children should know about the possibility of joining and using the library to extend their access to books of all types. Librarians are eager to help in this way, and the teacher and librarian to-gether can do much to help children to become regular borrowers. In order to stimulate interest in a book which you have either started to read or want to re-read, suggest that groups of children should paint big pictures of scenes or characters from the book. Hung around the room these create an added aware-ness of the book and increase children's interest in it.

Simple books for children to read

The book-list in Appendix 3 suggests books for children to read. In these we have looked for subject matter which arises from the children's own lives or which has been shown to interest them; and for language which is nearer to their own spoken language than is normally found in primers. We do not recommend reading books which have sacrificed all other aspects of written English to the careful introduction of graded vocabu-lary or 'sounds'. Nor would we recommend books which use constructions especially devised for little children, nor those which present an all-smiling, all-clean, all-smooth pseudo-middle class home-life.

Children's first books should lead them into child-ren's literature and to books generally; no child should have to say 'I can read all the reading books, now I want a *real* book'. This may represent some kind of progress but it is preferable that the transition from initial readers to children's literature should take place smoothly and imperceptibly.

Nursery rhymes

The traditional nursery rhymes still have a strong appeal to young children and some come to school knowing a wide selection. Apart from some specialised words, they have a simple basic vocabulary closely related to that of the Sentence Makers. They include a wider range of basic English grammatical patterns than any early reading books and they manage repetition without becoming boring.

There are, of course, many very attractive nursery rhyme books and you should try to add some of them to the class library but we felt that it is often difficult for a small child to find the rhyme he wants in a big book. So we have had 46 printed on cards that can be easily managed by very small children. They are intended primarily for a child to take at any convenient time to read alone or to other children or to an adult. They should be easily accessible in the classroom either in a box on the wall or on a low storage unit, and we would suggest that, rather than putting them all out at the beginning you should introduce them one at a time or change them from time to time. Take one or two rhymes with the class as often as possible, showing them where to start reading and following the lines along from left to right, top to bottom. If you can make more cards to include any special rhymes liked by your class this will add to the general store of reading material. The cards can be introduced with the help of the nursery rhyme record. On this the rhymes have been recorded in a variety of accents in order to stress the fact that there is no exclusively correct way of speaking English.

Teachers sometimes like to make a large wall version of a favourite rhyme so that a group of children can read it together. The illustrations for these wall charts should include as many points of information as possible. For instance, *Little boy blue* might be illustrated with pictures of sheep, a cow, a horn, etc., as well as the boy himself. The children should be encouraged to participate in the making of the pictures and to discuss the meanings of words that may well be strange to them.

When the children start to read the *Breakthrough* books they will find that the final page often includes a nursery rhyme; wherever possible we have tried to find a rhyme suited to the text of the book and in this way other rhymes have been added to the collection.

Longer singing rhymes have not been included in our sets of cards because they are best taken by the teacher; they have great value for a class or group, but it is difficult to set out rhymes such as *The Animals came in two by two* on a single card. Many of the longer rhymes and songs are on the record *Songs and Rhymes for the Teaching of English* by Julian Dakin (published by Longman) which has an accompanying pupil's book.

Reading aloud and intonation

Intonation is a very important feature of spoken language. In English a single sentence may have a number of different meanings according to the intonation given by the speaker. Fine shades of meaning such as polite contradiction, doubt or reservation can be expressed by altering the 'tune'.

Written language cannot indicate these patterns except through a few resources such as punctuation, underlining and italics. (Because of this, spoken language may be considered clearer and more precise than written language.) When children begin to learn to read and write they are, for the first time, separated from the spoken language by the silence of written language. Most children have great difficulty in producing the tunes of the sentence when reading aloud. Encourage them constantly to try to reproduce normal patterns of intonation in their reading and discuss with them the way in which you do it when you read to them. In the beginning some children will read aloud with a listing intonation, each word separated by a pause and given similar stress. Whenever possible read the sentence through to them afterwards, using the normal intonation and get them to repeat it. Children should be encouraged to read to each other, trying all the time to achieve a natural 'spoken' effect.

This task is much easier with sentences written by the

child in the first place, because he will know the 'tune' of the spoken form and can replace it fairly easily when he reads the written version aloud. In unfamiliar material the child should be encouraged to consider the context of the sentence he is reading; this will often give a clue to the intonation required. For example, a group lesson could be taken from time to time where one child reads and you say to him, 'In this story the witch is very angry, remember this when she speaks. Remember too that the children are very frightened.' Then see that the witch's words are read angrily and the children's in a scared and hesitant manner.

Some children may be nervous of reading aloud at first, even if they are quite fluent. It will be a great help if they have already had the opportunity to tell stories to other children and to hear other children telling stories to the group or class. Many children can tell stories, not only with full and natural intonation, but with dramatic effect, and if all the children are accustomed to doing this in front of the others, it will be easier for them later to read aloud. It may also help to let some children tape the stories they can read, and then play this to the class; the child is then able to listen critically to his own reading.

Accent and dialect

Infant School teachers are, on the whole, enlightened in their attitude towards accent and dialect. One clear sign of this is that they are concerned to encourage children to write and speak freely and are not given to correction of children's spoken language. In support of this we can say linguistically speaking, that the idea of 'pure' English is so much nonsense. *There are no dialects which can be considered sub-standard or wrong*; they differ from each other but they are all equally satisfactory means of communication.

The English speech community does, however, regard one dialect – Standard English – more highly than any other. This is a social and not a linguistic judgement. The word 'standard' as applied to 'standard English' means 'understood by all members of the English speech community'. It is not a standard of correctness in speech or writing, though it is the language of books and of classroom instruction (the latter will be in a variety of accents), and because of this it is necessary for all children to learn to use this dialect. But it is not appropriate to start teaching the child this explicitly as soon as he arrives at school.

In hearing the teacher speak, the child will be listening to standard dialect forms and, if some of these differ from his own, he will have to learn these. He does not have to replace his own dialect for one that is entirely different, but learns another for use in formal situations. More importantly, perhaps, he will learn to be understood by people over a wider area than that in which his own dialect is spoken.

If in speaking or in using the Sentence Maker and Stand, the child uses expressions such as 'I ain't got no milk', or 'we wasn't given none', try to accept this as the child's natural dialect form; the main concern is to encourage the child to speak and write without fear. With more advanced children differences in construction can be pointed out as *differences*, with no suggestion of a value judgement being involved; some may say 'I have no toys', others, 'I ain't got no toys'. At no time should a child be made to feel that his language is ugly, unacceptable or bad. Later in school life it may be necessary to explain the social prestige carried by some dialects of English, but the Infant School child should be learning to express himself in his own spoken or written language.

5

HANDWRITING

Introduction

By comparison with the other skills that a writer is called upon to use in composing sentences, handwriting is a low-level activity. Aesthetic considerations apart, it requires little beyond the development and control of fine muscular movements. However, this is no reason for leaving children to develop the skill unaided; for among the reluctant writer's difficulties, the failure to have mastered fluent handwriting (as well as fluent spelling) is a major stumbling block.

Success in written composition depends on the early acquisition of good handwriting and orderly, as opposed to random, spelling. Only when the writer has these skills well controlled is he able to concentrate on the higher intellectual tasks involved in communication and expression. When they appear together, slow and clumsy handwriting and insecure spelling are likely to ensure that a child will view any writing task with distaste and dismay.

Left to themselves, children will arrive at their own ways of making letter shapes. Some will be successful at this; others will quickly develop inconsistent and awkward movements which make their handwriting and its message obscure. Eventually this obscurity may become a mask for their uncertainty and fear. It will not be long before the habits they have taught themselves, become established and difficult to modify.

Their chief difficulties are likely to arise because:

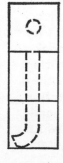

1 They are unaware of the way the writing space is divided into three. Unless we make this visible by means of ruled lines, and unless we describe the way each letter shape is related to the writing space, the child has to discover this for himself. Many children begin to

write with a total unawareness of the nature of the writing line.

2 They are unable to maintain one constant proportion to which the size of all letter shapes is related.

3 They are unaware that the writing line is horizontal and continuous across the page. They tend to have a number of horizontals at different levels.

4 They are uncertain of when to make clockwise or anti-clockwise movements.

5 They show little concern for the sometimes slight contrasts between certain letter shapes – for example: **h, n; a, d, g; v, y; i, j; l, i; d, cl.**

6 They make careless and incomplete letter shapes from which considerable ambiguity may arise.

7 They do not always sit in the most comfortable position for handwriting. They may write on their knees, or standing up, or cramped up into too small a space on an untidy table, or they may sit obliquely in relation to the paper and adjust their writing hand rather than their whole bodies.

The demands of handwriting are too great to be left to chance. They are not so great that careful early training will not make it possible for most children to produce smooth and consistent handwriting. Today none of us has to become obsessive about handwriting, as were our predecessors, in order to help our children to set workable standards in this for themselves.

Teaching handwriting

Soon after children come to school, and very soon after the literacy work starts, they will want to start writing for themselves. They have the same difficulties in understanding the nature and purpose of handwriting as they do in understanding the print in the class library books. They may describe their first attempts at handwriting as 'drawing names' or 'writing pictures'. When they are drawing they are usually making a representation of concrete objects; but when they begin to learn handwriting they must learn to make abstract shapes which are part of the conventions of the writing system.

About these they have no choice as they do in painting or drawing a picture.

The difference between printed materials and handwritten materials should be discussed.

It is likely that, just as babbling and experimenting with sound are necessary to the development of speech, scribbling and experimenting with parts of letter shapes are necessary to the development of the controls necessary for handwriting. Many children have done a great deal of scribbling at home or in a nursery group, but if they still seem to need to do this, let them use small blackboards and chalk, and do not try to direct them to the letter shapes too soon. Because the positions taken up by the hands and body are very different for a vertical (or near vertical) surface compared with those taken up for a horizontal one, children should have plenty of experience of 'horizontal scribble' too – let them practice making writing patterns with a stick in the sand, with paint brushes on newspaper, with crayons on paper and with any other media that suggest themselves. They need as much varied experience and practice as possible before they can concentrate on the letter shapes in detail and before they have defined their hand movements sufficiently.

When you feel that a small group is ready to start making letter shapes, explain that only a small number of movements will be needed and that if letters are taken part by part in an orderly way it is easier to see how they are made. Many children are naturally impatient and rush into wrong movements which may quickly become ingrained. A little extra time now will save them from the strain that handwriting often becomes for children later in their school lives.

In order to describe how letter shapes are made the children will need to understand certain technical terms such as *curved, clockwise, anti-clockwise, straight*. It is important for children to accept that letter shapes are made to a standard pattern. Later, when they have some mastery of the 26 lower-case shapes, they can be encouraged to discover variant forms of these in magazines or newspapers. You should help children to understand that this is the way we do it. We have no personal choice about the shapes on which our letters are based, and our aim is to help the children to produce these in the most comfortable and economic way.

Squares drawn like those in the diagram on page 49 are useful for demonstration purposes. Talk to the children about the way the writing line is arranged and let them suggest where they would place letter shapes without the three squares. If there are wooden letter shapes in the classroom, these will be useful for giving children experience of the positions of different letter shapes to one another.

Demonstrating handwriting

Take as an example, letter c. Prepare three large squares as in the diagram on page 49 and tell the children to watch the direction involved in making this letter shape. Write it for them so that they can see exactly what you are doing. While you are doing this slowly and clearly, describe exactly what is happening so that the children can learn to think about the process verbally as well as visually, and with the muscular experience of 'writing in the air'.

You might then say:
This is the way we write the letter c.
c is a curved letter.
My hand will go round this way.
I will write it in this square –
this is the middle square.
I start here.
Now I go round and down and up to here and stop.
Then I take my chalk off.
This is the letter c.
Can you see a space here?
It is nearly round but not quite,
that's why we say it's curved.
c is a curved letter. We always write it like this. I'll do it again.
Or the letter 'a':
This is the way we write the letter a.
a is a round letter with a straight line on one side.

When I make the round part, my hand will go round like this:
I will write it in this square, the middle square.
I start here.
Now I go round and down and up to the top.
That's the round bit of the letter, now I have to make the straight line on this side.
I go down to the bottom of the square and then stop.
I take my chalk off.
Can you see the curved part and the straight line?
This is how we make the letter **a**.
We always do it this way.

When you have shown the writing of a letter several times with a commentary, the children should be allowed to describe the process while you listen; later on some of the children may be able to demonstrate to you and the others, but make sure that they are getting the movements and description correct.

In order to write each letter many decisions have to be made:

1 In which square to put the pencil to start the letter off; all letters will begin in the middle square except for **b**, **f**, **h**, **k**, **l** and **t**, which all begin in the ascender square.
2 Whereabouts in the square the letter will actually start.
3 In which direction is the pencil to move? Clockwise or anti-clockwise?
4 Will the lines be straight or curved?
5 If there is to be a change of direction, when must it start? Before long it will be seen that letters such as **g** or **b** are made by changing direction and type of line (straight or curved) without lifting the pencil from the paper.

It is a very complicated process for a small child and each part of each letter must be taken several times in detail before the child can be expected to practise by himself. While they are practising the children will be going through what you have said in the demonstration, either to themselves or to each other. In this way they successfully internalise the process.

Once some of the children are ready to practise letter shapes paper may be prepared with three large

squares. These may be duplicated for use in the classroom. Later, when the children have gained more control, the size of the squares can be reduced to the size
of those in the diagram. A rubber stamp may be ordered
from a local manufacturer so that paper can be stamped
up by the children themselves whenever there is a need
for them to have practice of this kind.

Teaching which enables each child to think verbally,
visually and kinaesthetically about what he is doing
will provide him with the understanding he needs to
master the skill. The examples given of the making of
letter shapes are only to suggest how this might be
done. Each teacher will have her own way of approach-
ing the task with individual children and her own way
of meeting a variety of children's needs. We have been
concerned with the nature of the information which
will aid the development of clear, smooth and consistent
handwriting.

No child needs to be hurried into handwriting. The
use of the Sentence Maker ensures that each child can
use written language on his own before the handwriting process has been mastered, or even started.

6

KEEPING RECORDS

Many Infants' teachers record progress in reading by reference to the page number of a book in a series. This is not satisfactory for several reasons:

1 It encourages boasting among the successful children and a sense of failure among the slow.
2 It encourages children to become competitive.
3 The children are likely to be less interested in the books than they are in the desire to complete the reading of a series of books.
4 It is difficult to know how a page has been 'read'; it may have been memorised or the words may have been read aloud as separate items with no reference to meaning.
5 Very slow children are often stuck on the same page for a long time, they may lose all sense of what they are doing. They may even forget a page they could previously read or take so long to complete it that they have forgotten the beginning before they reach the end.

The processes involved in reading and writing are very complex and involve so many skills that, even assuming we could test every skill simply and effectively, keeping accurate records of each child's progress would be a full-time job.

Nevertheless it is important to have some record to which you can refer especially when children change teachers in the course of the year. So too, when class numbers are large, a careful record is the only way of ensuring that no child is overlooked or failing to make progress.

The use of the literacy materials produces two very important and quickly checked records for each child: the number of words in his Sentence Maker and the sentences which he has composed and which are written in his sentence book. If the sentence book is dated regularly it is possible to assess the way in which the child's sentences are developing and to see at a glance when this is not taking place.

Apart from these two built-in records additional information can be recorded. You may have a book or file with a page for each child or you may prefer to have a large sheet with the children listed down the side and the steps to be noted across the top. Then you need only tick or date the appropriate intersection. Information which could be included in this record is:

1 A note of abilities in working with the teacher's materials, such as: has started to join in sentence work, has started to recognise words (words known may be listed before a child has his own Sentence Maker), makes part sentences, makes acceptable sentences, can make a question, etc.

2 The date on which a child was given his Sentence Maker should always be recorded. After this, although a glance at a child's folder will show the words known, you may like to count his words monthly or each half term, or you may like to tick off entries such as, has 20 words, has 30 words.

3 From the sentence book in which you write the sentences composed by the child you will be able to get information about the kinds of constructions he is using and you may like to note landmarks in the progress already made. It is not easy to do this but you might record increases in sentence length and sentence complexity and the ability to produce more than one sentence.

4 The first use of the Word Maker should be noted and also the date on which the child first spells new words for himself. A record of the number of sound/symbol correspondences known by each child will quickly draw attention to who needs help in this aspect of the work.

5 You may like to note unobtrusively the books read by each child. This should be done in such a way that no child feels he must 'get through' and then discard the books he reads.

There are further ways in which it is possible to

record individual achievements. These suggestions will enable you to note the most important developments in the work of each child.

Suggested integration of work with *Breakthrough* materials

One way in which work with *Breakthrough* materials may be integrated is suggested on pages 58–64. This is set out under seven headings, under each of which one particular aspect of the work is introduced and suggestions made for its development.

As children are likely to begin working with the materials at different times throughout the year and to 'make differing rates of progress, it is important to ensure that those starting late do not miss anything that has been dealt with earlier. The plan on the following pages is an attempt to provide for such situations in a way that is both flexible and comprehensive. Our aim is to make it easier for you to ensure continuity in the work of every child in the class.

Not all that is set down in the suggestions will apply to all children: some will need to use the Magnet Board materials more frequently and over a longer period than others. Similarly work with the children's Sentence Makers will, for a time, continue alongside work with you on the teacher's Sentence Maker. All children, regardless of their readiness to begin using the other materials, will share the nursery rhymes, the story telling and story reading and will take part in discussions.

One aspect of the learning process applies to everything the children do, and is therefore excluded from the detailed suggestions that follow. This involves the need for children to talk and think about what they are doing. To do this to the best advantage they need to be able to use the special language which embodies the new ideas they are to meet. They need also to develop the ability to continue a line of thinking on their own; to ask questions when they are uncertain of something they have just met; to seek new information to clear away mystification or confusion; and to make and apply generalisations.

1 Magnet Board

Introduce a few of the figurines.
Show the children how to set them
up on the board and encourage the
children to make up stories about
them.

Begin to label some of the figurines –
give the children the words and see if
they can label correctly. Start with
single words *mum*, *dad*, etc.

Extend labelling to groups of words:
my mum, dad and the little baby, etc.

Teach children to match words used
for labelling back into the teacher's
Sentence Maker.

Extend further to the making of
sentences – *the baby is asleep*, etc.

Use the teacher's Stand in
conjunction with the Magnet Board
to make longer sentences.

Listen to children telling stories as
they use the Magnet Board and
encourage them to begin using the
past tense as, for example, in
beginning *Once upon a time there was*,
or, *One day a witch had a wicked
idea* . . .

2 Teacher's Sentence Maker and Stand

Put up the teacher's Sentence Maker
on the wall and have the words
ready for use with the first children
showing interest.

Very simple sentence work: *we are
the new children*, etc. should now
begin. Have the children's own
names ready.

Introduce negative and question
forms as soon as possible: *I am not a
boy. Am I a girl?* etc. Introduce the
question mark and the full stop soon
after the children have regularly
started to make questions and
answers.

Words common to most of the
children in the class, but not included
in the core vocabulary, should be
made for the teacher's Stand. A class
word store may be prepared for
seasonal words.

Extend the sentence work with the
introduction of new words as in *I am
a bad girl, my mum is pretty*, etc. Try
to introduce plurals: *I am in school,
we are in school*.

Encourage children to read their
sentences to other children, and to
listen to other children reading
theirs. Encourage them to read each
other's work. Record their first
sentences on a wall chart.

3 Children's Sentence Makers and Stands

4 The Word Maker

It will be helpful if you are able to make a teacher's Word Maker.

When a child knows from eight to twelve words he should be given his own Sentence Maker. He should be given his name card. The small Stand should have a plastic spot stuck to the left-hand end.
Teach the child how to use the Sentence Maker and Stand, how to put the words away, how to start their sentence near the spot on the Stand, where to put the Stand and Sentence Maker away, etc. If a child uses *mummy* or *mother* regularly see that he has the word as a substitute for *mum*.

When a child mistakes a word such as *dad* for *bad*, introduce the Word Maker. Draw attention to the over-all shape of the words and then to the shape of individual symbols.

Start the identification of initial consonant symbols and sounds in words. **b**, **m** make a good starting point. Teach children how to look through the symbols on the Word Maker systematically.

More children should be having their own Sentence Makers; make sure that they know all the words they have, and encourage the use of printed vocabulary as much as the personal words. Do not let children accumulate personal words faster than they can remember them.

Extend the discussion and comparison of the symbols in words; take a group of words such as *fish*, *shop*, *dish* and compare the symbol with those found in similar words round the room.

Help children to practise adding **-s**, **-ing** by using the Word Maker to show how it is done.

1 Magnet Board

Encourage the children to continue
with the Magnet Board, making up
stories about the situations shown;
faster children here can be a great
help to the slower ones.

If one or two children are good at
making up stories, let them occasionally do so for a small audience.
Discuss such topics as road safety,
catching a bus, driving a car, buying
sweets in the shop, doing things at
home. Introduce the fantasy figurines.

For the sake of slower children,
introduce a selection of the figurines
and set them up on the Magnet
Board one by one, as the story you
are telling unfolds. In this way it is
possible to introduce children to the
idea of characterisation and incident
in which time sequence and cause
and effect are developed. Encourage
children to share in the development
of a story.

2 Teacher's Sentence Maker and Stand

Encourage the children to operate
the stand and materials in groups of
two or three; see that they match the
words back into their correct places.

The use of the affixes may come up
naturally in the course of sentence
work. If it does not, introduce their
use. The plural **s** is probably the best
place to start, but **ing** may be
equally good; it does not matter
which is used first.

The children will need some help in
the use of more complex written
sentences. Take some group lessons
on using words other than *and* to
lengthen sentences and to make them
more interesting. Encourage use of
when, because, that, etc. *Our baby was
asleep* when *I got home; I couldn't go to
the party* because *I was sick; this is the
bird* that *flew away.*

The teacher's Stand and words can
also be used in connection with
project work and to write a sentence
which sums up some class discussion.
*Concorde flew today; Prince Charles is
Prince of Wales.*

3 Children's Sentence Makers and Stands

Try to keep pace with writing the children's sentences into their books; some of them will soon want to write for themselves. This should be done on loose paper. Keep the *sentence book* as a perfect record of the child's work.

Encourage the children to show each other their work and help children to use words such as *when*, *because*, *where* in the sentences they compose. Return to the teacher's Sentence Maker to do this.

The faster children will progress through the folder work on to writing for themselves, but they may need the folder for spelling reference, to help make a dictionary and to experiment with sentences after they have started to write. They may like to stand their Sentence Makers in front of them for reference.

4 The Word Maker

Help children to refine their word recognition technique by taking words from the Sentence Maker and making them in the Word Maker. Begin with words with few symbols.

The children should play several versions of spelling games using the Word Makers; for instance the changing of the initial, middle or final letters to make new words.

Discuss possible words like *geb*, *nop*, when they are made in the Word Maker.

When children start to write for themselves, they should try out the spelling of some of the new words before being told what it should be.

After children have ceased to need the Sentence Maker they should still be encouraged to work out spellings in the Word Maker and to play games based on the regular spelling patterns.

5 Nursery Rhyme Cards and Record

Put some of the Nursery Rhyme Cards out. Begin with the ones known to most of the children. Read them with the children, or sing them. Show the children that they can take a card out for themselves to look at and read.

The record 'Sally Go Round the Sun', which accompanies the Nursery Rhyme Cards is arranged in groups of about six rhymes. They may be played to the children as a set and appropriate cards shown at the same time.

Add a few or single cards, discussing new words, and showing the children the direction of the writing on the card. Encourage the children to read the cards on their own.

Rhymes that are very popular may be written on large sheets of paper and illustrated by the children, or single lines may be illustrated.

6 Books

Introduce the children to the book corner and from the very beginning read to the children from one of these books at least once a day. Stories should also be told, but the difference must be made clear.

At the story reading, start to discuss the differences between text and illustration and the direction of the writing; introduce and discuss terms like *word, space, beginning,* etc.

Encourage the children to look at books, and show them any new ones you put out.

Children may like to illustrate stories and make sentences up about them; put them round the room and point out words that are the same as those in the printed stories.

7 Miscellaneous

Put up notices in complete sentences around the room. Read them to the children.

Allow the children to scribble as well as draw on any surfaces suitable (blackboards, newspapers, etc.).

Put up the Weather Chart, discuss the weather and from now on make a sentence about it daily.

Write below the pictures and beside models made by the children, *exactly* what the child has said.

Put up the Sentences Chart, write some of the children's own sentences up and encourage them to read these. Children who are making sentences well should now have a book for you to write them in.

5 Nursery Rhyme Cards and Record

Add to the nursery rhyme collection any favourite skipping or traditional rhymes known to the children. Change the cards round sometimes and keep on reading them to the children.

Draw attention to the rhymes in the back of the books which are being introduced and read them to the children.

Nursery rhymes will continue as favourites with many children; go on reading them and encourage the faster children to read them —see that they read with correct intonation.

6 Books

Keep up at all times daily reading and discussion of the picture story books. Talk to the children about the public libraries.

Introduce *Breakthrough* readers to the children as stories. Introduce them about one every other day, starting with the yellow ones. Read them and discuss them, then leave them available for children in the book corner.

Children may make sentences in their Stands very similar to or the same as those in the readers; if so, show them the book and encourage them to read it from the printed text.

If children's own books have not already started, some should be made about now; they may be joint efforts centred round some event, or individual stories.

7 Miscellaneous

Talk to the children about handwriting. Some of them will be ready to start practising circles, clockwise and anticlockwise, etc.

When some children seem to be ready, start the detailed handwriting work with small groups.

By now the children should be making sentences in the weather chart without direct help.

At all times keep the notices round the room as new as possible and introduce the other charts (colour, number) when they seem to be appropriate.

Follow through the instructions for handwriting as suggested in this section. Soon some of the children will want to write their own sentences in their best book—let them try on sugar paper first.

5 Nursery Rhyme Cards and Record

Less well known songs and rhymes may be now introduced. At about this time children begin to enjoy nonsense rhymes, tongue twisters and puns. They are likely to show interest in experimenting with these forms for themselves. This should, of course, be encouraged alongside all the other forms they may use in their writing. The use of anonymous rhymes can be extended to include many kinds of poetry for children.

6 Books

Note the books which individual children have read, but let them re-read, as much as they like. Faster children should be encouraged to read to the slower, using the correct intonation and rhythm.

As children begin to read more confidently, direct their attention to selected primers from reading schemes (see Appendix 3) and the simplest picture story books.

7 Miscellaneous

Many different books should be made in the classroom and read frequently by and to the children.

Some children will begin to use reference books. *An abc for hungry girls and boys* and *About the house* were designed to serve as an introduction to reference works. Picture dictionaries and simple reference books should be available in the class library.

7

A NOTE ON PARENTS

In the schools in which the *Breakthrough* materials were first tried out, parents' meetings were held during the autumn term to explain what we were trying to do and how we hoped to achieve this. Parents were able to examine the materials and have their classroom use described. An important additional reason for the meeting was to discuss aspects of children's language learning and to enlist the co-operation of parents in the language development of their children. Such meetings are likely to be valuable to parents with children of school age and also to those with children in the nursery class.

Parent-teacher relations vary from school to school and parents' needs have to be met in a variety of ways according to local conditions. Some parent groups may be more interested in the theoretical aspects of their children's work while others like to know about practical work in the classroom. At home some parents teach their children to recite the alphabet and to make the shapes of capital letters. In the following note to parents there are suggestions for more useful things that they might do. Among these emphasis is given to the importance of adult-child conversation and discussion; to the benefits gained by the child who has stories read to him and told to him; to the importance of using the public library and of associating books with pleasure and with the child's expanding interests.

A suggested letter to parents

In suggesting that parents can help their children at home we are not for a moment thinking of homework, nor that time should be made available at home for work that should be done in school. Many parents however, wish to understand the purpose of what children are doing at school and to do all they can to support this at home. The following suggestions are of ways in which parents can do just this.

1 Speaking and listening. Before going to school your child is well on the way to mastering one of the hardest and most complicated tasks in life – learning to speak his (or her) language. Do not under-rate this tremendous achievement. Learning the spoken language does not stop at a certain age or when some level of proficiency is reached. Learning will continue most satisfactorily if your child shares your day to day conversation and if you answer his many questions as fully as possible. 'Children should be seen and not heard' is fortunately not often said today and the children who have had a chance to talk to their parents about everything that interests them start their school lives with a distinct advantage. This may seem unimportant to you; to your child it is vital.

2 Ways in which speech leads to reading and writing. Stories and plays seen on television or heard on radio can be very helpful in extending a child's interests. They can never replace story telling and story reading at home. There is nothing that can replace the warm, personal contact that exists between parent and child. Only in this way can children ask questions and have them answered, or ask for something to be repeated. After children have watched television programmes be ready to discuss these with them.

Do not neglect the old nursery rhymes and lullabies. Sometimes the words may seem to be nonsense, but children take great pleasure in them. They like the tunes, the rhyming and the repetitiveness of the rhymes.

Some people are very good at telling original stories. Others find it difficult. You can only try. The stories you tell need not be complicated or very grand. Some little event of the day will often do very well. If the story proves to be popular it can be repeated again and again. Small children have a great need to hear things often, because they do not understand everything the first time. From each repeat of a story they may learn something new.

3 Picture story books. When you are reading stories to children it is helpful if you explain what you are doing, showing them special words from time to time and explaining the difference between telling and reading a story. Many children believe that adults look at the pictures in a book and make up the story. They do not understand the significance of the printed words.

But what books should you read to your children? To begin with, any story that interests your child will do. The important thing is that story reading should be enjoyable. Children's tastes are very wide but you will have to experiment in order to find out what *your* child likes and dislikes.

You do not need to buy large numbers of children's books. There are Children's Libraries in every neighbourhood to which you should take the children. You will find the Children's Librarian very helpful.

In this way you can try out many books. If some of these become established favourites you can, perhaps, buy some of them. It is important for children to own some books.

4 Handwriting. Do not expect your children to write fluently too soon; it is a difficult skill to master. If your child is naturally left-handed do not try to change this but let him take the pencil in his hand in the most convenient and comfortable way.

Because we use capital letters less than lower case or 'small' letters, we do not teach capitals at first. An alphabet of the shape of the small letters we use is attached to this letter [to be supplied by the school]; the children learn to write their own names using these letters, writing a capital for the first letter only. If you would like to write underneath any pictures that they draw, or make little notices for their own room, please use these letter shapes.

5 Reading. Once your children start to read they will greatly enjoy reading to you and a little encouragement and praise from you is a great help.

6 To sum up. Talk, listen, discuss whenever you can: at home, when you take the children out locally or on

special outings, when visitors come; tell stories, repeat and sing rhymes, read stories from books, read notices in the streets. Let the children enjoy looking at and handling books: visit the library; give praise and encouragement to your children whenever they deserve it. These things may seem small in themselves but they are of the very greatest educational value and cannot take place wholly in school.

8

SUGGESTIONS FOR CHARTS

The Weather Chart, Colour Chart, Number Chart

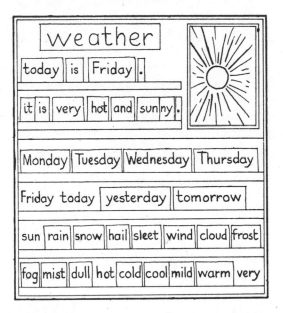

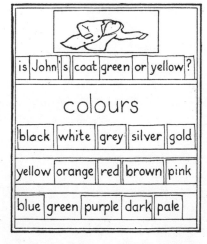

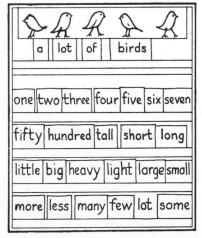

The illustrations show three possible uses for additional charts; a Weather Chart, a Colour Chart and a Chart to teach the children number words. They are made similarly to the model on page 71.

The Weather Chart should have pockets for storing the special weather words (such as *rain*, *snow*, etc.), a place where the children can form sentences (the equivalent of a stand) and a pocket made of clear plastic for illustrations. The sentences made in the Weather Chart may be recorded in a special book or class diary and illustrated.

The words in these charts should be made exactly the same size as the teacher's word cards. The children can then use the two sets of words together; the weather words when they are working with the teacher's materials, and the teacher's words when they are working with the Weather Chart. The sets of words can be easily distinguished if they are written in different colours; e.g. blue felt pen for the weather words, red for words from the Colour Chart and green for the number words, or they may be on different coloured manilla.

The words shown in the illustrations are no more than examples, you may have a selection better suited to the needs of your children.

A teachers' model of the Word Maker

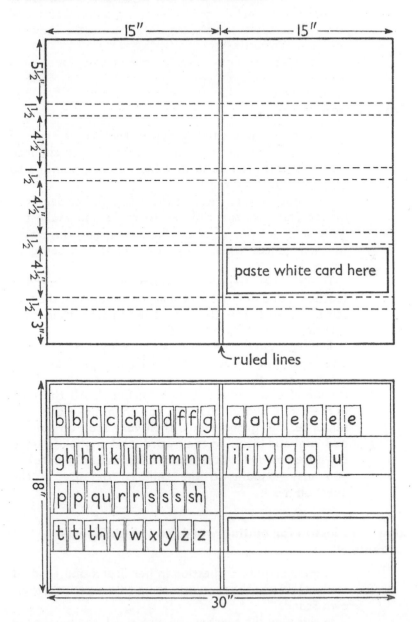

9

SPECIMEN LESSONS

Group lesson

The teacher has a small group in the literacy corner and puts on her Stand 'I am a teacher'. The children *read* this as a group and then individually, pointing to each word as they read.

The teacher then returns the words to her Sentence Maker and asks the children to come and make the same sentence one after another; returning the words to their places when they have made the sentence correctly.

The teacher then alters the sentence to 'am I a teacher?', and discusses the difference between the two sentences with the children. The children then take turns to make the sentence themselves again.

The teacher can then ask a child 'are you a teacher?'. The reply will probably be 'no I am a girl/boy'. The teacher can then remove the word 'teacher' from the stand and replace it with 'girl/boy'. All the girls in the group and all the boys can then make this new sentence. This group should then very soon be able to add 'big' and 'little' to their word stock to make 'I am a big/little boy/girl'. After this first lesson has been taken you may explain to the children the use of the question mark.

Suggested lesson for adding words to the children's vocabulary

The teacher puts a question in her Stand and reads it to the children; she then asks them to answer it in their own Stands.

In this way the teacher can also check the number of words a child has learnt by a sequence of questions and answers as follows:

Group 1: 14 words

Q. are you a boy or a girl?
A. I am a —
Q. are you big or little?
A. I am —

Q. are you good or bad?
A. I am —
Q. are you happy or sad?
A. I am —

Group 2: 10 new words

Q. do you watch television?
A. yes I watch television
(or yes I do)
no I don't watch tele-

vision (or no I don't)
Q. do you like television?
A. yes —
no —

Group 3: 9 new words

Q. do you go to school?
A. yes I go to school
Q. can you jump?

Q. can you walk?
A. yes I —
Q. can you run?
A. yes I —

A. yes I can jump
Q. can you jump up and
down?
A. yes I can
Q. can you skip?
A. yes I can
no I can't

Group 4: 13 new words

Q. do you go to bed at
night?
A. yes I —
Q. do you get up in the
morning?
A. yes I —
Q. do you have a dog at
home?
A. yes I have
no I haven't

Q. do you have a cat at
home?
A. yes I —
no I —
Q. do you have a bird at
home?
A. yes I —
no I —

Group 5: 7 new words plus words for title of story

Q. can you paint a picture
of your dog?
A. yes
no
Q. can you paint a picture
of your cat?
A. yes
no
Q. can you paint a picture
of your bird?
A. yes
no

Q. can you read a book?
A. yes
no
Q. can you write a story?
A. yes
no
Q. what story do you like
to read?
A. I like to read —

A lesson introducing words on the Magnet Board

The Magnet Board should be used to introduce words in their written form, but it should not be overloaded with words at any time.

The home can be indicated by the background furnishing and mum and dad can be placed in it. Give the children plenty of time to talk about what does and does not appear in their homes.

They should be allowed to move *mum* and *dad* round to what they consider to be suitable positions.

Then ask the children which of them has a baby at home. Ask someone who has, to place the baby in position, and then add the word. *brother* and *sister* can also be added on this basis unless it is apparent that the children have had enough new words already.

Six words in one setting, such as *mum, dad, home, baby, brother, sister*, are the maximum which should be taken at one time in this way, and plenty of discussion should accompany their introduction.

A lesson for a change

Children have a good sense of humour and quickly learn words such as *laugh* and *funny*.

The teacher has a group in the literacy corner and puts on her Stand: *I am a big cry baby*. She asks the children individually to read this and asks them if they really are big cry babies. The answers can be made in the children's own Stands and may be

    no I'm not *or*
    yes I am

Some children may wish to experiment further in their answers:

    I only cry sometimes
    I laugh I don't cry
    I cry when I'm sad
    I'm not a cry baby you are

The purpose of a lesson such as this is that two or three new words should be introduced and used by the children until they are fully familiar with them.

PART TWO: THE BACKGROUND

I

LITERACY AND THE ENGLISH INFANTS' SCHOOL

The changing classroom

The modern primary school teacher has a markedly different role in the classroom from that of her predecessors, not only in what she teaches but also in how she achieves this, especially in the relationships she establishes with her pupils. She has learned to recognise the importance of the social grouping within her class so that, when children are grouped for activity periods, they may choose to work with friends and not be compelled always to work with children chosen because of similar ability. Developments in learning theory have also affected modern teaching practice, so that children are less likely now to be regarded as passive objects to be stuffed with facts. Curricular reforms have usually preceded, and have revealed the necessity for, methodological reforms.

The theories in themselves, however, have no power to bring about educational change. Theoretical knowledge is important but the area of its effectiveness is related directly to the way it enables a teacher with forty children to teach with increased understanding. It is because this knowledge has had such an impact on individual teachers that they have effected this revolution.

Language and education

The demands made on the modern teacher are considerable and always increasing. She is asked to give the right guidance to each child at the right time; to make the children aware of their own progress; to make certain that the structure and sequence natural to the study are present. As M. A. K. Halliday writes:

Let us look briefly at language as a tool in education. . . . the new maths and the new science and all the other things that are new are making much higher demands on [the child's] language ability than what went before them. If we are helping him to find out for himself, structuring his experience in such a way as to provide progressive challenges to which his response can only be through continued conceptual development, as part of this process we have also to structure his experience of language. The capillary attraction school of thought, which maintains that all he needs is to be soaked in language, has held sway too long; it was an advance over the cushion-stuffing school to which it was a reaction, but like most reactions it was essentially negative in character. Teaching is neither filling holes nor benevolent inertia but guidance; the provision of environments in which learning can take place, in which there is order, progression and guidance. We know this well enough but have not yet applied it to language. It is not easy to know how, and let me not pretend that linguistics has the answers. But the answers will not be forthcoming except through the confrontation of professional linguistic understanding on the one hand and the professional knowledge of the educator on the other.[1]

Language, using the term in the broadest possible sense, is plainly of vital importance in the processes of teaching and learning. The spirit of Professor Halliday's words is often expressed by teachers when they say that 'every lesson is an English lesson'. The child needs language for the subjects of formal education and to help him to establish his own identity. Many children are well on the way to doing the latter before they reach school age, but others operate with a more or less restricted set of grammatical choices. If the child is to gain some understanding of himself and of his relationship to things and people he will require adequate language abilities.

This is an important (perhaps the most important) task of the Infant School but it is one which few teachers have been made aware of and which very few have been trained to undertake. It is easy to see how the problems of deprived children are overlooked, for it is far simpler in overcrowded classes to encourage the children whose backgrounds have already equipped them for learning and who can communicate effectively and structure their experience through language. It is greatly to the credit of those teachers who despite the difficulties also help the deprived.

The need for a balanced theory of literacy

The ways in which we have been using the word 'language' may be summarised as follows:

Language is that aspect of social behaviour by means of which we communicate with one another and organise our day to day living; and the ways in which we do this may be seen to be culturally determined.

At the same time language is private behaviour, for the expression of thoughts and feelings concerning ourselves and the world around us.

Language, both spoken and written, is patterned behaviour.

Many new approaches to the teaching of reading have been made by psychologists and educationalists. Infant School teachers will be familiar with the work of Gattegno's *Words in Colour*, Daniels' and Diack's *The Phonic Word Method*, Catherine Stern's *Children Discover Reading*, Stott's *Roads to Literacy*, the use of the Initial Teaching Alphabet and Jones' *Colour Story Reading*. There are many other new reading schemes, materials, apparatus, books, etc., published with the intention of providing the teacher with all she needs for teaching her children to read. It is difficult to sort out and evaluate these methods, approaches and materials. It is also difficult to evaluate much contemporary research in the teaching of reading. Very little of the great mass of material published on the subject is significant in contributing to a theory of literacy. Indeed much of it reflects the absence of a theory, and the absence of any awareness of the need for a theory. Consequently many relevant issues are ignored and emotional attitudes are established with little valid basis. Issues such as the 'rightness' of current methods of teaching reading are argued without establishing criteria by which the controversial areas can be identified and evaluated.

Perhaps the greatest need in the field of literacy teaching and learning is to develop a theory that will account for all that happens to a person in the process of his becoming literate. At present we know something of what the teacher does in her classroom, but we know all too little about how the pupil is reacting to, interpreting and understanding her procedures. This complex process needs to be described objectively in carefully defined and consistently used terms. Many of the terms used in research papers are not defined at all and are used loosely or even incorrectly. The use of the term 'phonetic' to describe the written language is a good example of a technical term being debased to relatively meaningless jargon. Such literacy theory as there is at the moment is known as reading theory, and there is no parallel writing theory, though schools in Great Britain are concerned with teaching both reading and writing. Writing is dealt with as part of the often fragmented courses of the Junior School, and reading, after the initial training in the Infants' School, is thought to proceed without much further help. Training in the teaching of literacy is not thought necessary for student teachers who are not going into the Infants' School.

We have already stated that a theory of literacy is the province of the linguist, the sociologist and the psychologist; yet reading research and reading theory in the twentieth century have been disproportionately dominated by psychologists. This dominance is reflected in the college of education courses for Infants' School teachers which generally include some examination of the psychology of the reading process but no linguistics and no sociology. None of these specialists alone can provide an adequate theory of literacy; in attempting to do this each is forced to work as an amateur (and too often at a trivial level) in the others' disciplines. A first step in achieving an adequate theory would be to break down the artificial boundaries surrounding each area of investigation.

By trying to describe the things the literate child has had to learn, and by suggesting ways of teaching these effectively in the classroom, we hope to give the successful teacher more insight into her success. If she can be equipped in this way she will be in a strong position to control the many variables present in the complex processes she is guiding. She will be able to interpret her role as instructor, evaluate methods and materials, and understand as much of what the child has to learn as of what she has to teach.

Unlike psychology, the contributions of linguistics, sociology and the study of children's literature have not yet been accepted either in the education of teachers or in research work. The search for a theory of literacy is a search for a way to bring all these studies together and to balance their contributions so that no one of them is isolated, over-emphasised or omitted.

Learning and failing to learn

Mental growth and learning are inseparable; the first is dependent on the second. It is now accepted that the old theory of learning as being a simple and regular progression from a to b to c, was a gross over-simplification. Rather, learning is an intermittent procedure and consequently growth takes place in spurts, followed by periods of consolidation and preparation for further advance; metaphorically it would be more accurate to describe growth as frog-hopping, rather than as a parade down a royal high-road.

The conditions under which learning and growth take place are also important. Liking and trusting the adults who help is obviously important; we do things for people we like more readily than for those we fear or distrust. Liking what we are doing is dependent on our understanding of why and how we are doing it. It is important for children to be aware of continuity of learning and for them to achieve some success at all stages. Learning is likely to be accompanied by temporary checks in progress. Making mistakes is a necessary component of any learning process; what the teacher must ensure is that the child learns to accept his mistakes and that he does this within a framework of help, reassurance and general progress. Success at each stage is possibly the greatest single stimulus to further effort. Extrinsic reward systems such as stars and marks may be successful at first but it very soon becomes apparent to the children themselves that the reward is likely to go to the same few children (and even for them it will cease to have incentive value). The system of giving rewards rests upon the rather capricious foundation of one adult's standards and opinions, rather than on the intrinsic merits of the work itself.

It is important for the teacher to know how a child is learning and to know what he is learning. In the beginning the five-year-old asks constantly for the help of his teacher. One sure sign that he is developing his own strategies and benefitting from your teaching is that he increasingly directs his cries for help to himself. Eventually he has to learn to work on his own with only his own thinking between him and the materials he is using. Only in this way will he adequately internalise the process that he is mastering. Because he understands what he is doing he enjoys his work and is pleased with the success that attends his efforts. In this way he will develop the practice of reinforcing his learning and will more easily remember what he has learned.

In his book *How Children Fail* John Holt writes:
Most children in school fail. Why do they fail? They fail because they are afraid, bored and confused. They are afraid, above all else, of failing, of disappointing or displeasing the many anxious adults around them, whose limitless hopes and expectations for them hang over their heads like clouds. They are bored because the things they are given to do and told to do in school are so trivial, so dull and make such limited and narrow demands on the wide spectrum of their intelligence, capabilities and talents. They are confused because most of the torrent of words that pours over them at school makes little or no sense, it often flatly contradicts other things they have been told, and hardly ever has any relation to

what they really know – to the rough model of reality they carry around in their minds.[2]

This fear of failing holds true for many children; for those who have ambitious parents and teachers; for those whose parents have no clear idea of what education is about; and for those whose parents have themselves been failures at school.

Literacy: reading *and* writing

'Reading' is a self-explanatory term, the word 'writing' is ambiguous; it may mean written language as opposed to spoken language, it may be used to mean a specific piece of prose, an individual performance ('a very clear piece of writing') or it may refer to the actual marks on the paper ('very neat writing'). When the term composing (or composition) is used here it will be employed to refer to that range of skills which contributes to the ability to produce written texts. Otherwise 'written language', 'the text', and 'handwriting' will be used to refer to the relevant aspect of written language under discussion.

Fluent readers and writers

Literacy may be regarded as the ability to operate effectively with the writing system of a language and we can show some of the abilities of a literate adult thus:

As a reader

Fluent reading (both silent and oral) for a wide range of purposes with a wide range of appropriate responses.

Wide range of reading techniques appropriate to the purpose among which are strategies for dealing with failure (e.g. ability to use a dictionary, to use reference books and to consult and discuss with other readers).

As writer

Ability to produce coherent written texts appropriate to a wide range of situations (e.g. domestic, workaday, educational, social and professional).

Ability to communicate within the range self-centred to subject-centred (poetry, letter-writing, technical writing, etc.).

As a reader

Ability to make critical evaluation of texts (to verify information, to recognise expressions of opinion and prejudice in the text, to assess the writer's attitudes, strategies and purpose).

Ability to add to his stock of knowledge by relating present reading to past experience.

As writer

Ability to predict readers' reactions and to write with a specific audience in mind; to write to produce a specified effect.

To anticipate reactions to the text (e.g. defining or not defining terms for lay or professional readership).

Ability to correct and amend original drafts and to examine self-produced material critically.

Ability to use appropriate forms of written language.

Reading skills

1 Word recognition – visual and visual representations of sounds and other elements of the language.
2 Structuring – using units above word – i.e. group, clause, sentence, paragraph.
3 Building up expectations and predictability.
4 Semantic interpretation – choice of meaning (of words, groups of words, sentences) according to author's intention.
5 Comprehension at cognitive and affective levels (in order for this to happen the reader must be able to share the knowledge and experience of the writer – i.e. they must have common ground from which the reader's experience may be enlarged).
6 Responding to what has been read from evidence provided by the experience of the reader in life and literature.
7 Evaluation – internal evidence and external criteria; from criteria derived from the external world.

Writing skills

1 Ability to think in large 'chunks' and hold thoughts in the mind while producing written language.
2 Skill with reproductive agency – hand or machine.

3 Ability to choose words, phrases, etc., and to evaluate their effectiveness and correct use.

4 Ability to reproduce orthographic patterns and read them back.

5 Choice of stylistic features, literary form. (For this the writer has to draw on his knowledge of all the texts he has read, on which he will model his own text, or use his own inventiveness to modify these or create new features. While young children are learning to write, they tend to have few models on which to base their writing and have not yet learned how to modify their speech habits to those appropriate to the written language. They tend therefore to write as they speak, in long groups of sentences connected by *and* or *then*.)

6 Ability to organise text – to take on role·that is involved in discourse; as story-teller to invent character, plot, situation, etc.

7 Ability to juxtapose elements of past experience, to invent new means of expression, to make use of new ideas, new information without plagiarising.

8 Structuring.

9 Response; development of self-criticism.

10 Evaluation; re-drafting.

11 Preparing a final draft.

What are our national standards in literacy?

Our present national achievement in literacy is difficult to assess accurately or objectively. There are two sources of information, objective testing by research workers and opinions expressed by teachers and employers (each of the latter is likely to sample small groups of people, whose statements have to be interpreted in the context of their special circumstances).

Complaints from employers about the low standards of literacy achieved by school-leavers may be prejudiced and unreliable. The 'good old days' were always golden; young people who are now likely to be working in responsible positions with scope for their talents would 20 years ago have been unemployed, or been employed in menial work in which any reference to their standards of literacy was irrelevant. However, the complaint is made that too many school-leavers can neither write clearly nor spell, and when this is substantiated, employers are not unfair if they consider that public education should have equipped the leaver with this basic tool. From time to time similar complaints are made by teachers. In his book *Middle School*, John Partridge[3] suggests that some five per cent of children in secondary modern schools leave almost illiterate and that a further 45 per cent find writing difficult. After 10 years at school these children have not learned how to spell, punctuate or construct simple sentences. A related complaint is made by the educationalist Keith Gardner about the earlier stages of education:

> I am haunted by a feeling that many educationalists have decided that in this modern age reading is an optional extra. There are so many other pleasurable things to do first. We can observe, record, evaluate; a few wooden cubes can unravel the mysteries of mathematics; we can dance, move, paint and make, coax music from a diatonic scale and watch television. . . . There is a town, a country, a universe waiting to be discovered, and somewhere along the line we might learn to read – if we are lucky.[4]

The painter Jack Taylor remembering his schooldays said recently:

> One teacher told me to spell the letter 'a'. I looked puzzled and the whole class started laughing at me. After that I didn't seem to learn much. I left school almost illiterate and I still have difficulty writing. I tend to write backwards, but I can read practically anything now.[5]

When we turn from expressions of opinion to objective testing, we find that since 1948 the Department of Education has conducted national surveys of reading standards in our schools. These show a steady rise in 'reading ability' as measured by the tests. We cannot answer precisely what is being measured as we do not have a clear idea of the complex processes that make up reading skills: to talk of assessing reading is like saying one is going to measure a motor-car: there are many systems to quantify and, unlike the car, we have no means of calibrating some of the essential ones. With that reservation we can go on to examine the findings of some of the national surveys. These show a marked nation-wide improvement (of some kind) since the war.

In 1964 an assessment of reading standards was made for the Plowden Report.[6] This notes the continuing improvement in reading ability (paragraph 585):

> Successive investigations into reading ability undertaken by the Department of Education from 1948 to 1964, make it clear that, despite the dismal reports that appear from time to time in the press, the standard of reading in the country as a whole has been going up steadily since the war. Children of eleven have advanced by an average of seventeen months since the first report was made, and backwardness now has a different connotation from that which it had in 1948. For this improvement the school can take much of the credit, but it does not dispose of all the questions asked about reading. The most important which remain are: what can be done to help the minority for whom learning to read is a slow business and for a few, never achieved? What use is made of the skill once it is acquired?

Another way of making the same comparisons is set down in the following extract from an unpublished lecture by John Sceats:

> But should we be too satisfied at such progress since 1948? For in that year schools were still suffering from the full effect of war-time disorganisation. The children being measured had endured the war, evacuation and very frequently, disruption of their schooling. Suppose we were to compare 1964 with 1938. This is impossible to do with any accuracy, as different tests were used; but one estimate suggests that the improvement at age eleven over these twenty-six years would only be about five months of reading age. But what a difference those years have seen in other ways – improved diet and general health, greater prosperity, a whole social revolution; not to mention the influence of TV, which tends, among other things,

to improve reading. This same estimate would show very little improvement at all with fifteen year olds.[7]

A formidable research document by Dr Joyce M. Morris for the National Foundation for Educational Research in England and Wales was published just before the Plowden Report.[8] It is a longitudinal investigation of children and deals with aspects of Dr Morris's previous report, *Reading in the Primary School*, and has three aims: '*extensive* studies in representative samples of primary schools, *intensive* studies in ten selected primary schools and *follow up* studies of selected children to the stage when they entered their first jobs.' Dr Morris's findings with respect to children in Kent are less comforting than the Department's, despite the fact that

> The reading attainment of Kent children in the final year of their primary course was above the average for the country as a whole. Kent was above the national average with regard to the percentage of children classified as having 'superior' reading ability.

We quote some of the conclusions of Dr Morris as reported in her book:

> ... at best, the chances of second year juniors with a reading problem eventually achieving average or normal competence is about one in eight, and at least half of them will remain very poor readers to the end of their school days.
> ... approximately sixteen per cent of the 'poor' readers hated reading in their third junior years, and nine per cent had abandoned all interest in books by the end of the primary course, and were planning future occupations for which they believed reading skill to be unnecessary.
> ... juniors who need the most encouragement to improve their reading standards were generally given the least in terms of the material conditions of learning and teaching provided for them at school and classroom level.
> ... the Kent enquiries do not provide sufficient evi-

dence to support advocates of either phonic or whole-word methods for introducing infants to reading.

. . . late beginners in reading are destined for secondary modern schools not only in fact but in the opinion of those responsible for their progress as juniors.

Whatever our national standards of literacy are now, they are not all they might be. The demands of education and the needs of society make the successful achievement of literacy imperative for all our children.

Success and the Infants' School

From the empirical investigations like Dr Morris's it seems that the Infant School establishes the patterns of success and failure that continue through the Junior School. Children must 'make it' in the Infant School and it is worth examining some of the reasons why this situation has arisen.

The educational system is administered in terms of chronological age. To grade classes by height or weight would give them a different composition but might be no less inappropriate. The immature, the slow, the disturbed, those in ill health and those who have had no background preparation for school work at home are at a disadvantage; they have only age in common with their class-mates. Their continuing need for Infant School teaching and an Infant School environment is ignored, except for the few who remain at the Infant School for a period of 'catching up'.

Teachers at Junior School level often assume that the pedagogic aims of the Infant School will have been achieved by the time the children come to them; they are not always trained to cope with the difficulties of the children who have not yet developed through the Infant School stages; nor does the Junior School ethos always encourage them to do so. We need most urgently to train our Junior teachers in techniques enabling them to deal with children of varying ability and who have reached varying stages of development, not all of which are those traditionally expected of Junior children.

The child's success or failure in the Infant School depends largely on his success or failure to acquire adequate linguistic skills. The environment of the children who fail usually lacks adequate stimulus for the full development of their resources in spoken language. They may lack, for example, a wide range of experiences of people, places and things; of affectionate, interested adults able to express themselves clearly in terms of answering, questioning, describing, explaining; of sharing curiosity and delight within an appropriate and consistent range of emotional states. We become adequate language users only when experience and language involve us, as children, in a share of adult company, as well as in that of our peers. Language deprivation is likely to be well established before the child enters the reception class of the Infant School. For such children the first years in school are critical for the future development of their ability to use spoken language. With every passing month of neglect the child's facility lessens and the likelihood of his learning to extend his use of language decreases.

It is for this reason that our best Primary Schools have replaced the silent classroom with activities during which talking and listening are at least as important as reading and writing, and where learning by doing and by observing has replaced teaching by rote. For many children their inadequacies are established and confirmed when they go to school, and it is small wonder that they grow up with a very muddled view of the nature of education and of their role in an apparently hostile society.

Bibliography

1 HALLIDAY, M. A. K., 'Language and Experience', a paper read to the Nursery School Association Conference on Children's Problems in Language. Harrogate, 20 May 1967. Published in 'The Place of Language', *Educational Review*, *Vol*. 20, No. 2, February 1968. School of Education, Birmingham University.

2 HOLT, JOHN, *How Children Fail*. Pitmans Publishing Corp., 1964.

3 PARTRIDGE, JOHN, *Middle School*. Gollancz, London, 1966.
4 GARDNER, KEITH, 'To read . . . or not to read', *U.K.R.A. Bulletin* 4, December 1966.
5 STURT-PENROSE, BARRIE, 'Primitives in Private', *Observer Colour Supplement*, 13 February 1966, pp. 18–19.
6 Central Advisory Council for Education (England), 'Children and Their Primary Schools'. H.M.S.O., 1967.
7 SCEATS, JOHN, from an unpublished lecture on the teaching of literacy. 1968.
8 MORRIS, JOYCE M., 'Standards of Progress in Reading', N.F.E.R. 1966. See also 'Reading in the Primary School', N.F.E.R. 1959.

2

THE THEORY UNDERLYING THE DESIGN AND USE OF THE SENTENCE MAKER AND THE WORD MAKER

The design of the Sentence Maker

When we came to plan materials for use in the classroom, we set out to provide children with the means whereby they might read *and* write from the beginning of their literacy learning. We were concerned to discover an appropriate way for the children to *produce* written language for themselves as well as providing special texts introducing them to the *reception* of written language. The emphasis we came to place on *production* in the first stages of learning to read and write is one of the places where we depart from the basic assumptions of traditional teaching methods in this field.

In many classrooms a variety of apparatus is used as an adjunct to a reading scheme. Some of it is commercially available and some is home-made by class teachers. In neither case is it always possible to avoid the criticism that some of these materials do not enable much learning to take place; some are not relevant to literacy learning; much of what *is* relevant tends to fragment the literacy process so that for the child it is difficult to relate the activities these involve to what he understands reading and writing to be about.

The rote learning of chosen vocabulary items and the use of flash cards is frequently an inevitable part of the traditional process of the teaching of reading:

. . . repetition – painstaking, conscientious repetition – is the key to the child's mastery of reading. Experts in child education have explored a number of different approaches to the teaching of reading; but whatever the approach, the actual establishing of the vocabulary in the memory is accompanied by repetition. By repetition, however, we do not mean the mere recitation of the same text. The art of teaching here is the art of making the same old thing acceptable, stimulating and infinitely varied.[1]

This attitude results in the production of primers where the texts consist of selected words repeated over and over: e.g.

Look, look! Look at the ball. I did get the ball. I did! I did! I did!

Any materials with which the child might, on his own, produce written language were less obvious to us, because there were no precedents for us to follow (although there are hints of what we proposed in the work of Sylvia Ashton Warner[2]). Materials for our purpose had to fulfil certain conditions:

1 They should be easy to use, easy to store and easy to maintain. With appropriate training Infants' School children achieve amazing standards of orderliness and self reliance. Our concern here was for the teacher who was to provide such training, and not for the children (many of whom show that they are able to use intricate classroom apparatus well if they are shown how to do this).

2 They should exclude from the skills involved in producing written language those concerned with handwriting and spelling. The typewriter, for example, will reproduce letter shapes but leaves the responsibility for correct spelling to the typist.

Our apparatus had to do this much, and provide spelling patterns as well.

3 Therefore the apparatus should be a word store and the items in it should be selected from those widely used by children of this age. It should make it possible for children to produce a very large number of sentences. There should also be provision for children to add words of their own choosing so that each child would draw on private experience in addition to that shared with other children.

4 In place of the line of typewritten letters the apparatus should provide a line of words held so that the child could carry it about the classroom. For this purpose the apparatus should include a stand which would make it possible for words from the store to be set up as a text.

One piece of apparatus we designed with these conditions in mind is the Sentence Maker. It consists of a triptych of card with the selection of words and affixes printed on two folds; the third fold is a blank store for the personal word collection of each child. Each fold has lines of pockets to hold cards on which the words are printed. Each word is also printed on the pocket so that when all the cards are in position they cover all the printed words on the material of the Sentence Maker itself; and whenever a word-card is removed from the pocket, the printed word is disclosed to mark the place of the card. The list is as follows:

> home mum dad television bed baby
> brother sister boy girl children friend
> teacher school picture story book house
> morning night day time birthday party
> cat dog shop car a a the the and very
> pretty big little good bad naughty some
> happy new all lot this I I my my they
> you me it we our he him his she her
> am is are was were will be been can
> do did work make made read write paint
> have has had come go came went said
> play walk run jump skip watch see saw
> want got get sleep kiss love like cry
> yes no es s s ed ing ? . not n't for
> down up by on to in out at of there
> why because when what with after but

Selection of the printed vocabulary

The words and parts of words printed on the left-hand and middle leaves of the Sentence Maker aim to anticipate the demand for such words that reception class children will make when they are writing. These do *not* comprise a list of 'key words', 'essential words' or items that the children must learn before they begin to write about the things they want to write about.

The Sentence Maker could have been left entirely blank. But two leaves have been printed so that when the child withdraws these words he will be able to match them back into their appropriate positions. In this way he is helped to master the processes of word recognition and spelling.

The inserts which duplicate the items on the printed leaves are supplied solely to save the teacher from having to write out 30 or 40 cards each with *mum*, *my*, *the*, etc.

When we were deciding which words to use we consulted a number of published word counts of the words used in the writing of Infants' School children, but we found no list that suited our needs perfectly. Our first list was based partly on published vocabulary counts, partly on our intuitions and partly on listening to children in the classroom. The affixes **-ed**, **-es**, **-ing**, **-n't** and **-s** were added to extend the basic stock by allowing the children to add inflexions simply and easily.

This first list was modified numbers of times in the light of classroom experience with the Sentence Makers. We have taken out many words that teachers found not specially useful and have added those that have been asked for most frequently. In this way we finalised a list to be used in a pilot trial.

In the course of our pilot-trial year we assembled a wide range of single sentences and texts made by children learning to use the Sentence Maker and fed these into the computer at The University of Birmingham. It was quite clear from the number of times each item was counted by the computer that some words were needed by every child (*I*, *my*, *a*, *to*, *the*, *and*, *is*, *am*). Our difficulty was to decide the additional words that would be needed by most children in most places and to exclude items special to any particular community. It was for this reason that we left out *garden*, *park* and *farm*. Obviously some decisions were hard to make; we eventually decided to include *brother* and *sister*, although some children have neither. The words *mum* and *dad* provided us with another problem again since children in different parts of the country use different words to refer to their mothers and fathers. Some children may say *mother*, *father*; *mam*, *pa*; *mammy*, *mummy*, *daddy*; *mum*, *dad*. We felt that we had to settle on one form and yet allow the children to use the form they were most familiar with. We therefore decided to print *mum* and *dad* in Sentence Makers and leave enough room for this to be altered to *mummy* and *daddy* or whatever the child used.

Our final selection was based mainly on the most frequent words found in the work of 5–6 year-old children who had used the materials. We modified this to include a range of grammatical words such as *who, what, were, there, by,* not all of which are easily used by some children. Inevitably there was a small number of words (about 20) which had to be chosen arbitrarily from the large number children had in fact used. Before finalising this group we asked the advice of teachers about those they thought it most useful to include. We were concerned that the final selection should also represent as many as possible of the major spelling patterns.

Stages in learning to use the Sentence Maker

In learning to use the Sentence Maker, some children seem to progress through a number of stages each marked by mastery of one part of written English. This description is an attempt to set these stages down in sequence, and results from our own observation of the learning patterns of the children in our first experimental group. It is offered as such and not as a statement of what will happen to all children in all schools using the materials. It is quite possible that we have omitted stages in this process or that what we have described as a 'stage in learning' is common only to a few children, or which some children will pass through rapidly.

1 Since the initial vocabulary has to be learned from its visual properties, it is hardly surprising that during the first stage many of the children simply list the words they recognise. Words such as *with, dad, boy, girl, children, go, Denis,* may be put into the Stand and read back to the teacher and talked about. In the specific example given here the child read two words incorrectly, *children* was read as *school* and *with* was not recognised on that occasion. There may seem to be

little here worthy of note; the child has merely learned to 'bark' at a given visual stimulus, not always the right bark at that; but he has learned to associate the black patterns on the cards with the sound patterns he makes with his mouth. Also, he read the word list from left to right showing awareness of one of the conventions of written English. It is also possible that the words in this example are not merely random selections; they may have been chosen as having, for the child, some semantic link.

2 The child begins to produce meaningful sentences, except that he omits words such as *the*, *to*, *a*, *is*, etc., thus producing a kind of telegraphese.

These omitted words have very little meaning by comparison with words like *mum*, *school*, *little*, etc. We describe the former as *grammatical* words and the latter as *lexical* words: the cement and the bricks as it were. The number of lexical words in the language is very large and that of grammatical words relatively small. This is perhaps easier to understand if we consider the following incomplete sentences: *the—go to—*. It is extremely difficult to complete this sentence by guessing at the omitted words; it could read: The *trains* go to *London*, The *students* go to *classes*, The *surpluses* go to *waste*, and so on. If, on the other hand, we had an incomplete sentence such as—*children—school*, there are fewer possible fillers for the missing words. *Little* children *read* at school. *Many* children *run* to school – there are a large number of possible ways to complete the sentence but proportionately fewer than in the first example. So with the sentence *the children go to school* the two words least likely to be correctly guessed are *children* and *school*; and these are the words that carry the highest amount of 'information'. Predictability and information may be seen here to be in inverse proportion.

When children begin to use the Sentence Makers they frequently begin by selecting the words with a high information content. We found that many children produced *baby little* or *children school* and read them to us as *The baby is little* or *The children go to school*, either not noticing that some words had been left out or considering the omitted words so unimportant that they could be added when reading the sentence aloud. Often, of course, such words can in fact be successfully guessed at by the reader, and added later (telegrams would have to be much longer than they are were it not for this characteristic of language). We found many partial sentences of this kind using only the words that carry the message (the lexical items), but we found the children produced no examples of sentences made wholly from grammatical words. That is to say that, while children will make sentences of the kind *mum home* for *My mum is at home*, the same sentence is never produced as *my is at* and read back as *My mum is at home*.

3 The children begin to realise that sentences of the *mum home* kind are incomplete and the missing words are added at the end to produce *mum home my is at*. At first sight this appears to be almost nonsensical but when asked the child will read aloud *my mum is at home*, inserting the missing words in their correct places and sometimes indicating them at the end of the Stand. Or the child may make the sentence on his Stand by selecting first the lexical items and then, taking up the grammatical items later, insert them in their correct places by moving the words selected first to make room for them. It should be clear by this stage that we are at least as interested in the mistakes the child makes as in his ability to produce acceptable sentences. It would be wrong to dismiss what appears to be a random selection of items when in fact it is organised in a way that is peculiar to a child at that stage in his development.

4 Often the children will produce partial sentences and we have noticed that in these cases there seems to be an emphasis on the noun phrase. Our children frequently made strings like *boy and girl*, *my mum and my dad and the children*, *my big teacher*, and *my baby*. These are simple labels, sometimes modified by adjectives and often preceded with the satisfying egocentric *my*. Sometimes we have found that children set up a nominal group first (e.g. *my little teacher*) and then say something about it, even though the normal grammatical ordering may be that the nominal group comes at the

end of the sentence (*my little teacher I love* instead of *I love my little teacher*). Traditional grammar would suggest that this is a confusion of subject and object; however, the child may feel that the object of the sentence, in this case *my little teacher*, is the real theme of the statement and knows that this can be shown by placing it first in the sentence sequence. (Compare *it's my little teacher I love*.)

All children try to get things right, and they arrange for themselves self-imposed practice deliberately to master a skill until they are able to use it with ease and understanding. By enabling the child to show us what he is doing in the process of producing an acceptable written sentence, we are more able to help him to gain control of written language. It is of little help to regard him either as 'able to write a sentence' or 'unable to write a sentence'. After examining his work we prefer to say that he is 'almost able to write a sentence' and then look positively at this 'almost', to see it in terms of praiseworthy achievement and of the help he still needs.

Many teachers will be well aware that children, in the early stages of learning a complex operation, revert to earlier mistakes: they may not be so aware of certain other stages we have observed. The common Infants' School practice of presenting written language always as complete and unchangeable will not allow these stages to manifest themselves. If the child is restricted to copying written language from a model, to writing over or below what the teacher has written (even though the child may have produced the sentence orally) he can display only his difficulties in motor skills. Later he may move on to forming the letters on the page with his pencil while holding the syntactic structure of the completed sentence in his mind. But the gap between success in writing sentences unaided and copying what someone else has written is great and it is not always easy to discover the sources of difficulty a child may encounter on the way. Neither can the teacher know accurately what to praise since she does not know what the child has done for himself.

Patterns in written English above the level of words

The recognition of the spelling patterns, that is, of the relationship between the marks on the page and the sounds we make with our mouths, is only the first step in breaking the code of an alphabetic writing system. It is possible that one could 'read' unfamiliar language by learning the rules of its writing system and converting the written marks into appropriate sounds. Children are sometimes found to do this. It would also be possible for a non-native to 'read' a novel in Czech for example, and pronounce the words in an acceptable fashion, without understanding a word of the text. The key to the substance of written language may be more or less easily learnt *but this is not a direct pass to the meaning behind the language*. To get beyond this it is necessary to understand the rules governing the patterns of the language from the smallest unit to the largest and those governing their meanings. We can set out some of the levels of patterning thus:

1 Ordering within words. If we consider the three symbols **p, n** and **i**, English allows us to order them only as **pin** or **nip**. The permutations **ipn, inp, npi** and **pni** are not possible words in written English.

2 Ordering words in phrases. The words *the, girls, pretty, three* and *little* are ordered, in English, as *the three pretty little girls* not as *the pretty three little girls, the little pretty three girls* nor any other combination.

3 Ordering parts of a clause. We can have:
the little boy saw him   but not *saw him the little boy*
six boys ran   but not *ran six boys*
one of them works hard but not *works hard one of them*
I gave it to him   but not *to him gave it I*

4 Ordering sentences of more than one clause. We can have:

they all got here on time, which rather surprised me
but not *which rather surprised me, they all got here on time*

How errors in understanding these patterns may appear in the classroom

Errors at all levels appear in the children's practice. Here are some examples of texts produced in one class on one particular day.

Written	Read as
school to go children little the	The little children go to school
my little girl school	My little girl is at school
the sun girl and boy play	(as written)
my friend go to school	My friend goes to school
teacher my es go school	My teacher goes to school
cat jump	The cat can jump
Franklin is my good baby little	Franklin is my good little baby
I go to run children school	(as written)
cat my home	My cat is at home
dad mum my my	My dad and my mum
go Cordelia school play with friend Anthea	Cordelia goes to school. I play with my friend Anthea
my dad was jumping happy	My dad was happy. He was jumping
children at school work happy	(as written)
we bad boy is see jump	(as written)
my teacher sad	My teacher is sad

Some of the difficulties in controlling all the processes involved in the act of composing written sentences are evidenced in these examples. There are no spelling mistakes, since the examples were made with small cards on which the words had already been printed, but some of the sentences have incorrect word order. The first example is written from right to left instead of in the conventional direction. In other examples words are omitted or they are out of order. Sometimes the sentence is structured so that there is only a hint of possible meaning.

How the Sentence Maker may help us to see problems being worked out

We found that the child's use of the Sentence Maker helped us to observe the outcome of some of the thinking and rethinking he might go through before reaching the solution to a problem. We strongly recommended that the teachers using the trial materials observed the children in order to note sources of difficulty as well as areas in which the children worked with confidence. The purpose of this can best be shown by describing one typical incident.

A group of four children were making sentences and the teacher was helping them. Another child, a boy aged four years nine months, joined them. He asked the teacher if he could join in, got his Sentence Maker and said 'Can I make a sentence now?' He selected four words and made, correctly, *I am a boy*. He read it to the teacher, studied his word store for a moment and asked 'Can I make "I am a big boy"?' He couldn't locate the word *big* so the teacher helped him find it. He placed the word *big* after the first word in the Stand so the sentence now read: *I big am a boy*. His teacher asked him to read it to her and he read quickly 'I am a big boy'. She said 'Look at the words and read them again.' The child began 'I am . . .' and stopped. 'Oh no, that's not right.' He found the word *am* in the sentence and took it out. He returned his attention to the Stand and tried to read what remained there, *I big a boy*, but knew it to be wrong and stopped again. He said 'I need another *am*' and it was obvious at this point that he was disorganised.

He had started by making something he was confident of: the sentence *I am a boy*. He tried to add to it the word *big* without first deciding where the adjective belonged in the text, realised he had done it incorrectly and, for a moment, was unable to sort out the problem. He picked up the word *am*, studied it for a while, looked at the words in the Stand and then suddenly beamed and said 'I see where it has gone wrong', and ordered the sentence very quickly to make *I am a big boy*.

This child was discovering, consciously for the first time, the importance of word order in written English. He was able to achieve the correct word order in spoken language without thinking about it but through his attempt to add a qualifier to a nominal in written English he was probably made partially conscious of this part of the grammar for the first time. Very similar difficulties may still be in evidence in the written work of some children in secondary schools, who continue to omit the grammatical words from their written sentences. The ordering of the sentence itself and the inclusion of all the necessary elements can be seen clearly by the children when they physically manipulate the words to form sentences.

The design of the Word Maker

A second piece of apparatus – the Word Maker – is of similar design to the Sentence Maker, except that it is smaller and has only two leaves. The pockets are printed with a range of written symbols. These are also printed on cards which are stored like the words – consonant symbols on the left hand fold of the Word Maker and vowel symbols on the right hand fold. These are arranged as follows:

Left Hand	Right Hand
b b c c ch d d f f g	a a a e e e e
gh h j k l l m m n n	i i y o o u
p p qu r r s s s	
sh t t th v w x y z z	two blank pockets in which to make and compare words.

The Word Maker in use

Many confused views of English orthography are held by many people and it is not unusual for it to be treated dismissively as having no rhyme nor reason to it. It is sometimes put forward as the main reason for the failure of some children to learn to read. It is certainly not the easiest orthography for the learner. However, all orthographies are abstract and complicated by nature and the way they reflect the language will be more or less complex *according to the nature of the language*, as well as to the historical and cultural aspects of its development.

It is more valuable to look positively at the orthography than to bemoan its shortcomings. It has more merits than are usually acknowledged and it is not yet proven that it need be the stumbling block to literacy learning that it is said to be. Pedagogical considerations have tended to blur the nature of the tasks that face the learner. At their best these considerations have never been able to present all the facts from which a linguistically sound model of the orthography could be built. In the main this has been left to the learner. In other circumstances (and some of these are outlined below) it is likely that mastering the orthography can be more successful for more people. It is, however, necessary to provide for continuity of development far beyond the Infants' School and this is not to be achieved merely by means of rote learning and ad hoc spelling tests. Children who are learning to think about the orthography and who are also highly motivated readers and writers are likely to succeed where the more unfortunate at present fail.

What is there to learn?

1 Listening to speech sounds – especially where there are differences in the speech sounds of the accents of teacher and children.

2 Learning to understand differences in the sets of speech sounds used by speakers with differing accents.

3 Learning how to think about the rules of the orthography and their exemplification. Learning how to discuss these and how to ask questions about them.

4 Learning the rules by proposing spelling patterns and noting how these may differ from conventional spelling. Learning to formulate rules as a result.

5 Learning spelling patterns as a reader: recognising spelling patterns and knowing how to pronounce the spoken words these reflect: learning how to add appropriate strong or weak stress to each word.

6 Learning spelling patterns as a writer: learning how to represent one's own pronunciation of words in spelling patterns: learning the *one visual form* for words or syllables which may have a number of weakly stressed spoken forms: remembering the list of words which belong to each spelling pattern – which means that, for *lexical* words, word meanings have to be associated with the spelling of homonyms.

7 Learning that letter shapes are not just geometric. They also have the special property derived from their position in space. Letter **n** is not letter n when it is upside-down: letter **f** is not letter f when turned horizontally through 180° – unlike a teapot which undergoes no change of *identity* with change in its position in space. The use of the separate symbols of the Word Maker allows children to *recognise letter shapes* and to experience some of the effects of moving these about. (Ideally these shapes should be in three dimensional form to give children the opportunity of arriving at the one and only spatial placement for each. To have provided these would however, have made the Word Maker cumbersome without adding significantly to its usefulness.) Some children will unconsciously make discoveries about letter shapes in space. They may do this better if it is discussed with the teacher.

The Word Maker also allows the child to try out spelling patterns without becoming 'committed' to the attempt in the way he would be if the word were written down. In the Word Maker an attempted spelling can be changed with no trace of the 'wrong' spelling remaining. It also enables the teacher to see the state of the child's knowledge of the orthography – the state of his model – and to see the outcome of his thinking. Because of this she is the more able to help where help is most needed.

Stages in the use of the Word Maker

1 Refining techniques of word recognition: replacing the child's random 'looking' by systematic awareness of all the units of which a word consists.
2 Learning the meaning of letter and of symbol.
3 Learning invariate consonant representations.
4 Learning alternative short and long vowel representations for simple vowel symbols a, e, i, y, o, u.
5 Learning that symbols may have more than one value. (Symbol **o** is one which needs to be dealt with early in any teaching programme because it involves some of the first words which children need to use. In order that they do not become confused without knowing why they *are* confused it is wise to give them the information that

some symbols are like this, leaving the details until later.)

6 Learning the meaning of *marker* symbols. It is likely to be of more use to children, in helping them to formulate the principles of the orthography, to give them a term like *marker*, than to give them one like *magic*. Referring to the final **e** marker in take, as the 'fairy e' or the 'magic e' is to take a condescending view of the nature and quality of the children's thinking.

7 Learning complex vowel symbols and beginning to collect the words which belong to each.

8 Learning the range of values these complex vowel symbols have. In words containing the vowel symbol **ea**, most words have one regular pronunciation as, for example, in *bead*. However, there are other pronunciations represented by this symbol and the words involved may be needed early in children's writing. These are all listed in the appropriate section in the spelling rules (pages 164–190).

9 Learning about syllable structure and consonant clusters.

10 Learning spellings of words each of which may be the only example of that spelling pattern. For example: *women, people, pretty*.

Teachers may find that children are helped in the task of remembering all the information they have to collect and systematise in their heads, if this is also collected and systematised in a series of spelling charts. These charts may be built up as children's knowledge grows. If each large page exemplifies one piece of information and is headed with a key word and its illustration to remind slower children (for example, a page to exemplify the symbol **sh** might start off with the word **fish** and a picture), this may become a reference point to which such children may return until they have achieved successful memorisation.

As such knowledge accumulates in the child's mind, he builds up expectations of what written words look like. As he becomes more and more fluent as a reader and writer he will make increasing use of these expectations (and similarly formed expectations of groups of words and clauses) in order to predict what is going to happen.

Bibliography

 1 MUNRO, R., *Janet and John Teacher's Manual*, James Nisbet, 1954.
 2 WARNER, SYLVIA ASHTON, *Teacher*, Penguin Books, 1966. Also the novel *Spinster* by the same author.

3

THE QUESTION OF FORMALITY

What is formal?

It is important to sort out two kinds of *order* in the teaching and learning of literacy. The first kind is the *order within the subject* itself and the second is *the order imposed by the teacher* on how and what she will teach. The subject, the English writing system and the English language which it reflects, are formally ordered and patterned in many ways. Similarly, a maths or science specialist would regard his subject as being ordered. We cannot say: 'As we are having a free-activity period now, we will add two beads to two beads and call the total seven'. Nor can we say: 'We are concerned to write creatively and therefore you may write from right to left' (or we would say these things only under very special circumstances). The writing system has rules. The process of becoming literate involves their acquisition and use.

The way in which the formal rules are taught and learned are decisions for the individual teacher and her class. However, we believe that this learning and teaching will be more effective and pleasant if the teacher uses the methods of the modern Infants' School. It is not our intention to impose any kind of formality *on the methods and approaches* to teaching of initial literacy. *What she is teaching* does that and, though she is free to ignore the patterns in the writing system, a knowledge of them will help her to understand the kinds of problems children encounter in their literacy learning and will make her assistance more effective.

Restrictions in children's writing: writing under the children's pictures and restrictiveness

It is the practice in many Infants' Schools for the teacher to write, under pictures the children have drawn or painted, whatever the children have said in describing them. This is interesting and stimulating for the children and a great encouragement to them to discuss the motives which gave rise to the picture – its content, the colours used or some particular features of its design and composition. Much of this may be difficult to write down and at best will be like the labelling found under photographs in an album: 'Blue boats sailing', 'A big elephant doing his washing', 'A funny man in the circus'. At its worst it will appear as stereotyped answers to the question 'What is it?' or 'What is it about?', 'it's a house', 'here is a little girl', 'this is a cowboy'. Further, it must be borne in mind that the child is still operating in the spoken language only. He has not in any sense *written* anything and although he may be able to read back what the teacher has written at that moment, may very often not remember exactly what it was a few days later.

It is, therefore, important to know what this activity in fact achieves. It is part of the general work in interesting the children in written words and in showing them that their spoken comments can be recorded for others to read when they are not there to explain their work themselves. The teacher is still doing all the work and the child, who has little knowledge of how to record thought and speech is given no direct experience of this for himself.

Teachers who have not used the Sentence Makers have sometimes said that their use would seem likely to confine the children's creative and imaginative writing because the vocabulary is so limited. This indicates some confusion between the spoken and written language. At a time when a child is starting to read and write he has almost no knowledge of the written medium. He is restricted only by his ignorance of it. His spoken language is rich and imaginative and for some time will continue to be well in advance of his ability to use the written language. For this reason, work with the Sentence Maker has to begin humbly; what restrictiveness there is in what the child does with it is in the nature of his learning situation and *not* in the design of the Sentence Maker. As an aid to learning it offers him ways of using the language that are open-ended. It allows him to make English sentences for himself. The time he takes to reach a mastery of written language will depend on many factors, none of which has anything to do with the Sentence Maker. But if in using it he is encouraged to know both his limitations and his operational freedom, he will have built a sound framework for himself by the time he feels secure enough to abandon its use.

Creativity and language

Our concern has been to make it possible for children to read and to produce natural, meaningful language. We have tried to avoid the charge laid at the door of earlier linguistic approaches to the teaching of reading and writing that the written language presented to the children was far removed from their interests and from their own linguistic resources, and different in kind from that found beyond the schoolroom. It was not difficult to avoid using the language of the 'put the pin in the tin bin, Min' construction which was designed to direct the child's attention to the form of written words.

It was much more difficult to write sentences that were 'right' in all respects. We have found that children wrote sentences which seemed to us at first sight to have little to do with conventional notions of 'what children want to write about'. Thirty years ago many Infants' teachers were convinced that small children wanted to hear about elves, gnomes and fairies. The current emphasis on 'creativity' in the Infant School is a reflection of the ascendency of 'private' writing found in some Junior Schools. Writing of this kind is important and, since it is highly motivated, is very useful in any literacy programme; but it must not be considered the *only* valid use for the child's newly acquired skills.

The children in our experimental classes made many sentences like *my dad said to me you can go upstairs* where there seemed to be little motivation for writing in terms of 'the interests of the child'. To the modern Infants' teacher, accustomed to the 'reading through experience' approach there may seem to be an artificiality about the sentence and a confirmation of her suspicions about the lack of 'child-centredness' in this particular linguistic approach to the teaching of literacy. This fear is seen to be unfounded when the child fills in the context for us. (With this particular example the little girl told us 'My dad said to me "You can go upstairs" yesterday, because he didn't want me downstairs all the time. I was sitting in my nanny's sitting room watching the telly and my dad didn't want my television on. I was watching Secret Squirrel and my my dad wanted to watch a film.') At the stage when children are not able to produce more than one sentence this one sentence is often only a part of a 'story' the child has in his head and the sentence he produces is often a dramatic highlight from it.

The term 'creative writing' is seldom defined; it is more frequently illustrated by examples from children's own writing and from which a definition may be arrived at by guesswork. It is essential to understand very much more about the creativity involved in the diverse ways in which a child is expected to use language. Literary creativity is only a part of a much wider and less obvious creativity which is inherent in the linguistic resources of every individual. There is a tendency in all of us to regard language, and especially spoken language, as being in some way the poor relation of literature; literary oriented English courses dominate all others in the schools; literary rather than oral models are taken as the norm. These views exert an influence down into the Infants' School so that certain kinds of imaginative writing come to be regarded as the crowning product of teaching. The unexpected or the startling and original phrase certainly encourages a teacher to believe that her children are gaining in sensitivity and the ability to examine experience and organise it coherently. *But these peaks must not blind her to the essentially creative nature of the language use of all small children – the creativity that is exhibited, for example, each time a child participates in a speech act.*

In the classroom, children using *Breakthrough* materials produce many examples of what might be described as 'creative writing' long before they have the motor skills to form the letters for themselves.

It is most important to note that the child who tells his teacher an imaginative story which she subsequently writes down for him is not engaged in creative *writing*; but in creative speaking. He is not producing written language in any sense. His teacher is doing that for him.

The quality of the imaginative writing done by the children will depend very much upon the teacher, on the kind of stories she reads and tells to the children and on the way she encourages them to strike out on their own with the equipment she has given them.

The *Breakthrough* materials do encourage the children to write about the things that concern them most and this, in itself, is likely to lead to the production of what is commonly recognised as 'creative writing' (the more so when the teacher discusses all kinds of events with the class, reads them stories, poems and rhymes and encourages them to share their writing with each other).

4

THE ENGLISH WRITING SYSTEM

Introduction

Leonardo da Vinci discussed the absurdity of attempting to represent the natural world by painting on a flat surface, of attempting to depict what the eye sees 'realistically' in three dimensions by arranging selected blobs, lines and patches of colour on a two-dimensional surface. Equally we could say that it is absurd to attempt to render the complex patterns of noise, gesture and face-pulling that constitute spoken language merely by making marks on a surface; reducing the dynamism of speech to a spatial system of scratches. Children learning to read find the concept of a writing system puzzling and magical. To the four-year-old one of the inexplicable wonders of the adult world is the intricate horizontal rows of black swirls, spots, lines and curves that his mother looks at when reading him his bedtime story.

Where English fits in among the writing systems of the world

The choices open to the makers of orthographies are strictly limited; it may be helpful to set these out so as to indicate where the English writing system fits into the range of types of orthographies of the literate communities of the world. There are three main kinds of writing systems: alphabetic, syllabic and morphemic.

Alphabetic writing systems can be subdivided into two further categories – phonetic writing systems and phonological writing systems.

There is only *one* phonetic writing system; it uses the alphabet of the International Phonetics Association to represent different sounds by distinctly different written symbols and a system of diacritics and other marks. *This is the only writing system that attempts to*

Alphabetic

A small number of letter shapes from which a larger number of written symbols may be made in order that for each distinctive speech sound there shall be at least one corresponding written symbol. It may include punctuation, diacritics, stress marks and other distinguishing marks. The base of the system is an alphabet. Greek, English, French, German, Italian, Spanish, Russian and Bulgarian are examples of language communities using alphabetic writing systems.

Syllabic

A large number of characters each of which represents a separate syllable of the spoken language. The base of the system is a syllabary. Cuneiform of ancient Mesopotamia and Japanese are examples of syllabic writing systems.

Morphemic

A very large number of characters each of which represents separate morphemes; that is words or affixes (the way in which we write Arabic numerals in English is an example: the character 3 symbolises the word *three*). The base of such a system is a list of logograms or hieroglyphics. Chinese is a morphemic writing system.

represent spoken language on paper as accurately and objectively as possible. It is not used by any language community as a medium of communication, it is used by phoneticians as a precise means of representing on paper the pronunciation of the spoken form of any and all human languages.

Most of the writing systems with which we are familiar use an alphabet and are *phonological*. Greek, English, French, German, Italian, Spanish, Russian, Bulgarian, etc., are all *phonological* writing systems. They do not attempt to represent spoken language precisely and accurately; they do try to represent each distinctive speech sound of the given language. Abercrombie describes this difference in the following way:

> The full range of possible human phonetic performance is very wide. . . . Only a selection . . . is put to use by the speakers of any single language – a selection, moreover, which is not only limited, but

different in very many (one might almost say nearly all) respects from the selection used by speakers of every other language. It is this selection from the full general human phonetic range which is formed into the patterns which carry the particular language. The selection, and the patterns into which it is formed, constitute the *phonology* of the language. The phonology of every language is peculiar to that language, and different from that of every other language.[1]

It is the items of this phonology that tend to be represented or symbolised in the writing system.

The demands an orthography makes on the learner, especially during the initial stages, vary from orthography to orthography, from writing system to writing system. In Chinese, the load is particularly heavy; each word picture or logogram must be learned individually. In Spanish or Swahili orthography where the 'fit' of the writing system to the sound system is nearer the perfection that is demanded of our own, the learning load is *comparatively* light. Our own orthography, like that of the French, for example, is somewhere between the two; both in number of letter shapes and in the way the rules of the orthography combine the written symbols into words. But it must be remembered that orthographies serve the needs of individual languages which differ from one another in almost all respects: in their sound systems, their grammar, their vocabulary, and their social and cultural uses.

Our writing system

The English writing system has had a complicated history. Its Anglo-Saxon forerunner evolved out of an adaption of that used by Latin. Changes in the spoken language encouraged the Old English scribes to alter the writing system, but it ceased to have the closeness of 'fit' with which it began. Since Caxton's day, printing has resulted in the spread of literacy and with this has developed strong opposition to any change in a writing system of great complexity.

The reasons for this complexity are to be found in the way that the writing system of Old English was gradually overlaid not only with the effects of changes in pronunciation, but also with the effects of the Norman Conquest and the absorption of words and orthographic conventions from Norman French. In periods of colonial expansion words derived from many other languages were added: and during the English Renaissance words of Greek and Latin origin as well. The orthographic forms of these additions give clues to their derivation.

The idea that the writing system should be absolutely uniform, with a single correct spelling for every word, regardless of personal mannerisms and preferences and local variations in pronunciation, gradually took form and gained acceptance during the eighteenth century. By 1755, when Johnson published his famous dictionary, he could set up as one of his objectives to adjust 'the orthography, which has been to this time unsettled and fortuitous'.[2]

Today our writing system is put to a great variety of uses. It is the medium of literary works, and of an ever expanding range of texts both technical and non-technical. The needs of education are served by a wide variety of pedagogical texts and by drawing upon the immense storehouse of printed material now available. Many people have helped to make the orthography what it is today and the result is a work of wayward genius. Against the reproaches hurled at it, we would protest that, when looked at in the right way, it is not as bad as it is made out to be. It is complex, and imperfect, but it is not chaotic.

Some opinions of English spelling

Language has been defined as patterned behaviour and 'patterned' is applicable to both the spoken and written forms. Were our orthography as un-patterned as Shaw and some other spelling reformers have suggested, few of us would manage to learn it. However, it has inconsistencies which might be removed: the orthography is not a sacred cow, except to those who, like Lord Chesterfield, believe that a mastery of English spelling is a sure mark of the educated man: 'I must tell you', he wrote to his son in 1750, 'that orthography, in the true sense of the word, is so absolutely necessary for a man of letters, or a gentleman, that one false spelling may bring ridicule upon him for the rest of his life. And I know a man of quality who never recovered the ridicule of having spelled *wholesome* without the w.'

On the problems concerning spelling reform Francis writes:

> It is possible to devise a system for English which eliminates many inconsistencies of the present system without sacrificing its position as an interdialectal standard. It is not an easy task, and it would require a virtually encyclopaedic knowledge of dialect variation in English and considerable ingenuity in working out a coordinated system that would be consistent in itself as well as compatible with all important regional variants. Most proposals for 'simplifying' or 'reforming' English spelling come from people who lack this kind of knowledge; they are usually well-intentioned amateurs . . . . But in spite of sometimes quite powerful advocacy and considerable expenditure of money [proposed changes] have not caught on. It is probably safe to predict that they never will.[3]

A. C. Gimson makes clear how cumbersome it would be if we were to write with phonetic accuracy, where *every* difference in the speech sounds we utter (phonemes) was represented on paper:

> . . . Today, few would seriously maintain that our writing should present an exact record of our speech. If this were the case, we could simply adopt for our reform the principles of the International Phonetic Alphabet, with its roman-based letters for phonemes. The resultant form of writing would be a kind of phonetic transcription, providing us with a great deal more information than we need for the visual comprehension of our own language. Either we would quickly learn to ignore in reading and writing a great proportion of the written cues, or our speed in

reading and writing would be greatly reduced. (It is worth noting that our present imperfect writing system permits a speed of silent reading at least double that of normal speech.) Moreover since each of us speaks English in a different way and is capable of producing the same utterance with different phonemic and prosodic components according to the style of speech, we would each have our own individual way of spelling the same English language. . . .[4]

Differences between spoken and written language

The English writing system excludes certain features of spoken language such as stress and intonation except to the extent that we are able, in writing, to indicate intonational features by means of italic forms and by the use of the question mark. Otherwise stress and intonation are features that have to be added in reading aloud, and without any indication in the orthography of how this should be done. Many people do this indifferently well and almost all young children when they first begin to read do so as though they were reading a list of words. They do not use the intonation proper to the spoken form of the sentences they are reproducing. This is caused in part by the fact that they are over-conscious of words and less aware of linguistic units larger than words.

The writing system does however represent some less obvious aspects of the language. Its directionality is a representation in spatial terms of the temporal flow of speech. In the latter we have no choice; in the former the writing systems of the world demonstrate that some choice is available in the way space may be used to represent time. In Arabic the direction is from right to left; in English from left to right. There are other possibilities. We accept one convention of a number of possible conventions and five-year-old children (and for that matter, illiterates of any age) do not know which is ours until they are given the opportunity to learn about it.

The writing system also disregards the flow and pause of normal speech, and uses letter space to separate letters, word space to separate words and sentence space (and full stops) to separate sentences. In the initial stages of becoming literate this presents difficulties. The child, whose perceptions are keenly tuned to receiving and producing spoken language in continuous flowing stretches, has, for the first time, to deal with the familiar in an unfamiliar guise. Our materials attempt (among other things) to introduce the child to these features of the writing system and to enable him to understand them and talk about them.

The writing system also provides for paragraph spacing and verse spacing, both of which reflect aspects of the organisation of meaning on the page.

Summary

Our writing system may be described as follows:
1 It is an alphabetic writing system. The basic stock of letters is 26. Each of these has two shapes – a lower case and an upper case – with many variants of these shapes in both printed and hand-written texts.
2 The writing system uses letter space to separate letters and word space to separate words. Sentence, paragraph and verse space are also used.
3 The writing system has punctuation marks for marking certain linguistic boundaries.
4 *Italic* variation of letter forms is used to draw attention to part of a text and to mark stress.
5 A small set of logograms (signs standing for whole words) such as the ampersand (&), numerals, those indicating currency units (£, $, etc.) and contractions such as Mr, Mrs and Dr are used.
6 The apostrophe is used to indicate possessives (John's) and contractions (it's).
7 It is worth noting that the English writing system alone of all European writing systems, uses no *accent marks* (cf. French and the use of accent in French orthography).

Speech and writing – some major differences

1 Speech consists of sound made by the speaker's vocal organs and received by his listeners' ears. Written

language consists of marks on a writing surface made by a writing tool and received by the eyes. The child does not hear the sounds of spoken language as separate units. The written language shows the *letters* as distinct shapes on the page, and *words* are isolated by the use of word spaces.

2 Spoken language occurs in time while written symbols occupy linear space. Further, written symbols are ordered lines from left to right and the lines are read from the top of any given page to the bottom.

3 The production of spoken sounds may be seen and felt as complex movements of the speech organs. The writing of symbols is not part of a child's experience in the same way. When the child begins to learn to read and write, his motor control is likely to be at a stage near to scribbling and it is tempting to compare this with the early stages in learning to speak – that of babbling. But scribbling results, not only in a later ability to form the limited set of letter shapes used in writing, but also in the ability to represent an unlimited range of objects and pictorial patterns in drawing and painting.

4 Speech is almost always a social act. Most speech acts are dialogues and the situations which give rise to them are shaped unconsciously by the speakers. Writing, while it is being produced, is almost always a solitary act, in which the writer is isolated from both people and situations. He is alone with his ideas and his ability to express these in written language.

5 There are many features of spoken language which are ignored in written language. Intonation, for example, is of considerable importance in English grammar and many shades of meaning are carried by intonation patterns. The written language has only very limited resources with which to indicate these patterns and relatively infrequent use is made of them. Similarly, rhythm, stress, the weak forms of words and other features of spoken language appear, if at all, only in the most restricted way in written language.

6 Both spoken language and written language are complex in organisation and patterning. However, they differ in substance (spoken sounds as against written marks); in the organs used to produce and receive them

(the organs of speech and hearing as against those of writing and reading); in form (the lexis – vocabulary – and grammar of spoken language are different in many respects from those of written language); and in the situations and purposes for which each is used.

7 Both spoken language and written language are symbolic; but written language is, as Vygotsky puts it, 'a second degree of symbolisation'. That is to say, in writing, as opposed to speech, we are entirely removed from the objects and situations to which the language refers. Vygotsky goes on to state: 'Our studies show that it is the abstract quality of written language that is the main stumbling block, not the underdevelopment of small muscles or any other mechanical obstacles'.[5]

Some features of the orthography

We have stated that our English writing system is an alphabetic one which reflects the sounds and other elements of the language. Many attempts to describe the orthography have been made, including some made by linguists, in which it is considered to be full of inconsistencies and exceptions to the rules. These results do not arise entirely from the inadequacy of the orthography but in part from inadequate observation or incomplete descriptions of its structure. They stem basically from the deep-rooted belief that, in the English orthography, the letters of the alphabet represent the sounds of the spoken language simply and directly, and that this is all that the orthography does. In languages like Spanish, Italian, Czech, Finnish and Swahili phonological items and written symbols correspond or 'fit' more obviously than they do in French, English or German. In the latter orthographies the visual symbols not only give information about the sounds of the words (the noises we make with our mouths), they also give other kinds of information. English orthography does this in a number of ways:

1 It distinguishes grammatical items from lexical items (e.g., *in* and *inn*).

2 It distinguishes, by spelling patterns, words from differ-

ent sources such as Graeco/Roman, Romance languages (e.g., *photograph*, *nation*, *century*)
3 It has special rules for writing proper names.
4 It presents syllables in the same way whether they are stressed or unstressed and thus provides one constant visual form for each.
5 It distinguishes many words that may sound the same in the spoken language.
6 It distinguishes monosyllables from polysyllables.

An adequate account of English orthography must account for these features and all the others it may have. When this has been done and the patterns of the orthography have been described exhaustively there will be relatively little data that can be labelled 'exception to the rules', or 'inconsistent'.

Changes in spoken and written language

The spoken language is changing continuously. In comparison to changes in the written language these take place relatively quickly, but never so fast as to be disturbing to any one generation of speakers It is only by comparing the speech of our day to that of our grandparents and great grandparents that we become aware of how much the spoken language has changed. Changes in the written language, especially where the printing press is the over-riding method of reproduction, take place very slowly. When handwriting (and the handwriting of a relatively few literate people at that) was the sole means of production of written English, it was possible (at least in theory) to vary orthographic symbols from time to time to make them conform to variations in pronunciation. With the advent of the printing press the desirability of having a standard orthography gradually prevailed over those who were still able to exercise some choice over how they should spell. The dictionary makers (the lexicographers) finally provided a standard spelling. 'Universal literacy' has since then ensured that the orthography remains 'petrified', and this situation has been maintained. It continues to be so maintained by the millions of people whose internalised mastery of it is deeply embedded in their mental processes and by the presence of a great body of printed texts.

The writing system represents one dialect of English

The pronunciation of words used in examples in this book is no more than the one we ourselves know best. It is one of the many pronunciations found in southern England. Other sections of the English speaking community have very different pronunciations. The differences are most apparent in speakers' vowel systems. If written language attempted to represent separately the speech of speakers in London, Wales, Lancashire, America and Australia, for instance, written communication over the dialect and accent boundaries would break down – unless everyone was prepared to learn many varying forms for the same word. The orthography to be found in the poems of Robert Burns, for example, presents many difficulties to speakers of other dialects. Our present orthography, Received Orthography as it were, enables us all to write in a standard form but leaves to each of us the job of learning a set of correspondence rules by means of which each of us relates his own pronunciation to its standard orthographic representation.

Some misconceptions

The confusion of written language with spoken language affects the teaching of initial literacy. We see the muddle evidenced in the child who asks 'what does this letter say?', in the teacher's complaint 'he doesn't know his sounds' and in the parent who boasts that her child 'can say all his letters'. Letters obviously cannot 'say' anything. They are visual cues which correspond to sounds the reader may or may not choose to make; they are silent marks on a page. One feels sympathy for the confused child who thought herself deaf because she was unable to hear any noise at all when her teachers asked her 'what does this letter say?'. This particular child remembers clearly the relief she felt when, at the age of eight, she first realised that letters say nothing and that her anxious straining to listen for the whispers from the marks on the page was unnecessary. Many of us use idiomatic expressions similar to this: 'what does it say in the papers?', 'what the papers say' and so on. Generally these are harmless enough and acceptable in a figurative sense but, if used in school, they can give rise to misunderstandings and confusion in the minds of very young children.

The teacher who says 'he doesn't know his sounds' does not in fact mean this, but rather that the child doesn't yet know the *relationships* between the marks on the page and the sounds of the spoken language. Virtually all five-year-olds 'know their sounds' in the sense that they can reproduce all the noises of their mother tongue (albeit in the accent of their neighbourhood dialect). They may be quite unable to perceive sounds in isolation. At this age the ability to do so varies very much from child to child. The parent's boast that her child can 'say all his letters' is referring, of course, to his ability to recite all the letters of the alphabet in their correct sequence. This was a task required of all children some years ago, but now wisely regarded as being of little importance in the initial stages of learning to read and write. Some parents still imagine that this is the way to begin and so teach their children the names of the letters of the alphabet and their shapes (often in upper case forms) in the traditional alphabetic order. They are supported by the knowledge that there are many ABC books which do this and by the memories of their own schooldays when this happened to them. Teachers, however, know well the confusions that this may cause if it is not taught with care and prefer to teach the children the names of the letters a little later in their school life, when this knowledge is needed for labelling the letters. Later still, when reference books begin to be used, alphabetic order has some purpose.

When the time comes for teachers to discuss with children the role that letters play in the writing system, the letter names are useful labels; but knowing the names and order of the letters of the alphabet is of very limited help in giving children an understanding of written English. It puzzles children to be told that 'when

they know their letters they will be able to read';
and it is not true. The following statements by two five-
year-olds show something of the effects of this
attitude.

ANDREW: [some words] are unusual. They're fun-
nier than others – not the same letters as you say
them in [sic]. 'Play' – you shouldn't have the 'y'. It
makes the 'ā' say 'a'. Like 'cornflakes' – you shouldn't
have the 'e', you should have a 'x' in its place. . . .
Mrs E. [the teacher] wondered how I knew 'me'. It
was one we hadn't had before. It's a wonder they
don't put 'ē' instead of 'e'. (How could they do that?)
Write mE, or they could put two e's.
TOMMY: 't' and 'h' together is hard. And 'this' with
a small 't'. You'd think it's a different sort of word.[6]

Some notes on the phoneme; or why you can't say letter L says 'l'

In attempting to describe the relationship between the
marks on the paper and the sounds we make we might
choose to work from the written symbols (such as **c, th,
igh,** etc.) to all the different sounds they represent; or
we might try to show how the different sounds we
produce are represented in the orthography (the **k**
sound in **c**at, so**c**er, **ch**aos, in**k**, ex**c**eed, **q**uick and so
on). Both descriptions would imply that there was a
comparatively small number of sounds that can be
related to a small set of written marks. However, a
listener who is trained to discern minute differences
between sounds can make finer and finer distinctions
and identify an almost infinite set of types of sounds
occurring in the speech of any individual.

So far we have talked as though there were only one
l sound or one **p** sound, etc. If we listen closely to a
speaker, however, and over-ride our expectations, it is
possible to notice variations within each single 'sound'.
The five words

look, bu̧lb, health, apple, play

share a common 'sound' that we can refer to as **l**. But
if we listen carefully to the **l** sound in each word we may

begin to notice unexpected differences. Comparing the first two words we may notice that the first has what Is traditionally described as a clear I, in contrast to the dark I of the second word. The two Is do *not* sound the same. If the dark I is transferred to the beginning of the first word, look, its 'darkness' is more obvious. We have what sounds like a Scottish pronunciation of the word and Scots do, in fact, use a dark I at the beginning of syllables where Standard Southern English speakers use a clear I sound. The two sounds are quite different in an absolute sense. In health the I sound, in addition to being dark, may be made with the tip of the tongue just touching the teeth, instead of the ridge of gum just above the teeth, as is the case in look and bulb. The I in apple forms a syllable on its own and, in the final example, the I sound is partially unvoiced in many accents of English in contrast with the voiced I in the other words. These differences can be shown by means of instrumental analysis: a machine that draws 'pictures' of utterances would probably show different patternings at the place of the I sound in each of the five words.

Linguists are aware of these differences; the native speaker is not; but the fact that the five I sounds are associated with a single letter, is paralleled by the way in which the linguist brings together all the members of such a 'family of sounds' and refers to this family as a *phoneme*. Thus we can talk of the I phoneme in connection with the example we have outlined. It is not easy to describe exactly what is meant by the term phoneme; the sounds in the above five English words are different, yet functionally related; yet we cannot strictly refer to them as a single sound for they are a group of sounds.

The implications of this for the teacher are not hard to see. She cannot point to the letter I in each of the five words and say that 'letter L says I' (she would probably use the 'dark I'). A phonetician, a modern Henry Higgins, would need to say that when we read these five words we produce, at the appropriate place, sounds which may be represented by the symbols:

(a) ḻ (b) ƚ (c) ḻ (d) ḷ (e) ḻ

I in look – ḻ

I in bulb – ƚ

I in health – ḻ

I in apple – ḷ

I in play – ḻ

In this way, the linguist is able to classify into phonemes the multitudinous sounds which are produced in the speech exchanges taking place about us. There is evidence that very small children are aware of distinctions between one sound and another in any one phoneme and may find difficulty in relating groups of sounds to their corresponding orthographic symbols. When children learn to read and write they must learn to associate several different sounds with each written symbol; several kinds of I with one written symbol I. It is hard for us to know how difficult a child might find this problem because we have long since learned the correspondence between, for example, groups of I phonemes and a single I symbol and are no longer aware of the range of differences in the former.

We could, theoretically, have had distinctively different symbols for each different sound in the phoneme (five different symbols for the Is we have discussed) and the orthography might have been extended enormously to cover all the differences between all the sounds we make in spoken language. This is not done because the differences within one family of sounds are not *CONTRASTIVE*; that is, the use of any one of these does not create a different word. The word *look* could be pronounced with a dark I at the beginning and it would remain the same word *look*; whereas if we change the initial sound to a **b** we have the word *book* instead of *look*.

Bibliography

1 ABERCROMBIE, DAVID, *Elements of General Phonetics*, Edinburgh University Press, 1967.
2 FRANCIS, W. NELSON, *The English Language*. The English Universities Press, London, 1967.
3 FRANCIS, W. NELSON, op. cit.
4 GIMSON, A. C., 'The Transmission of Language', in Quirk, Randolph, *The Use of English* with supplements by A. C. Gimson and J. Warburg, Longman, 2nd edition, 1968.
5 VYGOTSKY, L. S., *Thought and Language*. Edited and translated by Eugenia Haufmann and Gertrude Vakar, M.I.T., 1962, p. 98–9.
6 REID, JESSIE F., 'Learning to Think About Reading,' in *Educational Research* 9 No. 1, pp. 56–62.

5

LETTERS, SYMBOLS AND SOUNDS

Letters and symbols

The traditional view of English spelling is based on a belief that the 21 consonant letters and 5 vowel letters *as letters* are the sole units which make it work. This alphabetic view overlooks the facts in many ways. The **y** in **baby** is listed among the consonant letters, yet it certainly does not represent a consonant sound in that spoken word. Similarly in the word **language** the letter **u** represents the sound **w** although it is known as a vowel letter; in the word **have** the final letter **e** represents nothing in the spoken word **hav**, and in a word like **through** seven letters are needed to represent the three sounds that make up that spoken word.

Obviously, any attempt to describe English spelling with reference to letters (which have already been placed in consonant and vowel lists) does not allow the facts to emerge. For this reason it is necessary to put forward an alternative.

The 26 letters of our alphabet form the small basic set of named shapes from which we build our words. Traditionally, the letters have been described as having three attributes:

1 Shape: there are two forms of each letter – lower case or 'small' letters and upper case or 'capital' letters.
2 Name: letter names are still traditional labels. Many children learn them at home, and also learn their order in the alphabet. The majority of symbols derived from the letters of the alphabet have no names and thus in the spelling of words the names of the letters are called in sequence; but not in a way which delineates functional spelling units.
3 Power or value: traditionally letters are held to have correspondences with the sounds of the language. Children's ABCs seek to list these, and exemplify them

arbitrarily. In this way incomplete and often misleading information about the orthography is presented to children.

Letters as such have no power or value in our definition. From the basic stock of 26 letters a very large number of symbols is derived, and it is these that have power or value. In some cases letters and symbols are identical. The letter **p** forms the symbol **p** in **p**in, and if all symbols were similar, it would not perhaps be necessary to introduce such a distinction. However, letter **p** and letter **h** together form the symbol **ph** in **ph**oto. Thus it is **p** and **ph** (as symbols) that have power. *It is only when letters have become symbols that they represent certain elements of the language.*

The most important elements of the language represented by written symbols are *speech sounds*. The way in which symbols do this is complex partly because the way in which our speech sounds are organised is itself complex and partly because we inherit a writing system which represented the spoken language of five hundred years ago: since then inconsistencies have increased in number, but despite this our spelling is highly patterned and much of it very consistent.

Symbols also represent distinctions between lexical words (*inn* for example) and grammatical words (*in*); they provide different spellings for words which sound alike (*site, sight, cite* for example but not in a few words like *read, lead, wound*); they maintain one form for words which are reduced in speech as in *where ev you bin* (spoken), and *where have you been* (written). The suffix **s** represents the plural (as in boys) the possessive (as in boy's and boys') differing only in the use of the apostrophe. Yet the spoken equivalent may have one of three pronunciations. Thus we find boy**s** with a **z** sound, *p*et**s** with an **s** sound and hou**ses** with **iz**. They represent distinctions in words which when spoken have only slight differences (compare *summer dresses* and *some addresses* and *a peal of* and *appeal of*); they represent visual patterns which have no counterpart in the spoken language (the symbol **c** for instance cannot be given a sound correspondence until we know what the symbols around it are – if we have **c**at, musi**c**, **c**ell, **c**ity, we can then give it the value hard **c**, or soft **c**; and in the word **love** the final **e** makes no reference to the spoken language and this must be understood just as a visual pattern).

It is, therefore, important that in teaching about spelling we do not attempt to relate symbols only to sounds, as in traditional phonic teaching. There is much more than this to teach.

Summary

Written symbols are derived from a set of letters numbering 26.

The list of symbols that are derived from these is very large (approximately 300) and these consitute a visual representation of the sounds of the language.

Some symbols correspond regularly to one sound, e.g. **sh** is pronounced sh, in **ship**. Other symbols correspond to more than one sound. An important aspect of orthographic patterning is that by which the sound correspondence of one symbol is affected by another symbol.

In addition, symbols also give information about grammatical and lexical features. For example **past** is differentiated from **passed** though both sound alike. Similarly the verb **be** is differentiated from the noun **bee**.

For a full analysis of letters, symbols and sounds, see Appendices I and 2.

6

THE SPELLING RULES

Introduction

During the period in which children are learning to remember the look of whole words and becoming aware of spelling, there are many occasions in which they are faced either with the result of forgetfulness or with a word new to their pens. In such circumstances they are in the position of having to apply what little they know explicitly of the rules. They are likely to do this by way of examples of the way the rules have applied to words they know. (They may well not be able yet to express a rule as such.) Their difficulty in spelling words on their own stems from the fact that they may be able to think of several possible ways in which to represent a spoken word without knowing certainly which way is the accepted spelling.

Differences in pronunciation among children as well as differences in their awareness of spelling patterns combine to produce a wide range of attempts to spell. These are likely to be revealing of the child's model of the spelling rules and are worth discussing.

In order to help teachers and children to a sympathetic understanding of English spelling we have included a section on the common values that we attribute to written symbols, and one on some of the most basic spelling rules by means of which symbols are combined to make written English words (see Appendix I). In teaching it is not possible to apply these separately: values and rules go together.

Children will learn to spell more successfully if they are interested in and curious about language, if they are using written language that is meaningful and memorable to them, if they are using it frequently and for many purposes. From the beginning, they have to use words which involve many spelling rules and have, gradually, to make the mastery of these part of their linguistic stock-in-trade. In order that they may become coherent about how to spell, they should be encouraged to ask questions about things that puzzle them and to discuss the way they find the rules are working. Through talk of this kind they will come to understand the conventional and sometimes arbitrary nature of the way the language is represented on paper.

The argument is not that spelling matters more than sense (as it seemed in the dark dictation days); spelling does matter – whether it be your spelling, my spelling or our spelling. It matters because without it we cannot begin to write at all. Were we to have a host of private orthographies used by public writers, communication by means of the printed word would be that much more difficult.

Children's success in school depends upon how far the written language has become a major influence in their linguistic development. And that being so, we have no choice but to help them to a mastery of spelling. As teachers we are likely to do this better (as in everything pertaining to language), the more aware we are of the nature of the activity.

A writer's fluency depends on many factors. Mastery of the low level skills of handwriting (or typing) and spelling enable him to give a large part of his conscious mind to the aspects of his writing, its style and content, which are unique to him. Fluency in handwriting and spelling give the writer greater freedom to convey a particular message in a particular way. They do not guarantee creativity, originality, the use of the imagination or unmuddled thinking.

In Appendix 1 (p. 164) teachers will find some notes on English spelling. These consist of a description of some of the spelling rules, lists of common spelling patterns and information about speech sounds and written symbols. This is intended for reference only.

Children are likely to use words according to their interests and not in any pre-ordained order. It is not suggested that they should be taught directly from this Appendix, but rather that this is the kind of knowledge that they will eventually acquire. It is for the teacher to decide *how* and *when*. She is not free to decide *what*.

7

HOW SHOULD SPELLING RULES BE TAUGHT?

From the work of linguists, such as Weir and Venezky, it is clear that the orthography is highly systematic and it is likely that the fluent reader has an internalised model of the orthography, although he is unlikely to be able to say what this model looks like. It is part of the domain of the linguist to investigate the written language and to describe the patterns to be found in it, whereas it is for the psychologist to say how internalisation of these patterns takes place within the individual reader/writer. The traditional spelling lesson is an ad hoc approach to the task of internalisation and one which, for lack of awareness of the working of the orthography, falls back on random procedures and on rote learning. This statement implies that materials should be presented in sequences, but not necessarily from the most simple to the most complex; indeed 'simple' is not likely to be meaningful when applied to an item such as the sound/symbol correspondence of the vowel in **mat** where, in the orthography, the rules involve us in knowing how the environment of such a letter affects its sound/symbol correspondence. Take for example the letter **a** in

⟨mat⟩
⟨mate⟩
⟨matting⟩
⟨mating⟩

One possible teaching approach – the alphabetic approach – orders the teaching of the patterns from what is thought of as most simple to most complex. Another approach – the differentiation approach – generalises the set of environments which specifies the vowel values rather than specifying each vowel value separately.

There are good reasons for suggesting that the alternation between short and long vowel values should be taken together, with the environments in which these occur. As Venezky writes:

> Whether or not a child first learning to read can handle this task probably depends upon the pedagogy employed. The potential generalisation derived from the differentiation approach, however, certainly is greater than that from the simple-sequence method.[1]

We have attempted to present no more than the major patterns to be found in English orthography and which exemplify its systematic nature.

Learning the spelling rules

Traditional ideas about orthography are as false as the school grammars of the past, and traditional approaches used with children of five years of age sometimes wrap up the facts in whimsy. This makes it no easier for children and indeed may well get in the way of the child's understanding. A model of the orthography that is derived from teaching about 'letters that hold hands' or 'letters at the front door of a word' is not likely to be of much use to the child who must attempt to understand the principles underlying the spelling-to-pronunciation rules.

Many children, despite all that we tell them about our orthography (as in many other linguistic matters), do as their teachers did before them; they internalise a model of the orthography that works. That is to say, they can spell correctly when they write and recognise spelling patterns correctly when they read. Many other children make sense of it slowly and indifferently, and some retain throughout their lives so rudimentary a model that they are never able to do much about reading and writing. For them English teaching is remembered only in terms of dreaded spelling tests and composition, and reading books that bored and confused them. They make up a large part of the population that believes it was 'never any good at English'.

However, it would be an overstatement of the case to suggest that inadequate teaching of the orthography alone is at the crux of the problem. Children may master the orthographic substance and the recognition of words and grammatical structures in a way that far outstrips their understanding of a text. 'Barking at print' was a frequent and well justified way of expressing criticism of the old phonic teaching. For implicit in it was the belief that this skill was all that mattered. We cannot get far *without* the ability to decode the substance of written language; equally we cannot get far *with* it alone. It alone in no way guarantees anyone the ability to read with understanding, with purpose and enjoyment.

All attempts to ease the child into the orthography are worthless if, in the end, they do not enable him to internalise a model that works. With English orthography this will be likely to take several years to master (one is tempted to say that it *should* take several years, for there are many words that are out of reach of the young child, and some of these will certainly involve patterns and conventions not needed until he has had considerable experience of written language). There is another reason for the time taken to become 'a good speller'. Spelling patterns and all the other conventions of the writing system are only one part of the overall patterning with which the learner is dealing. They do not exist separately from the patterns of grammar, vocabulary and meaning and if the child does not also have some understanding of the larger issues from the beginning, the more difficult it will be for him to become literate.

Learning to become a reader and writer

The child has to learn a new role as a reader and a writer, and the new uses to which he can put his language. He must accept the 'silence' of the new medium in place of the 'noise' of spoken language; the slowness with which it is produced, in place of the ease and speed with which he speaks: he must learn to become skilled in a private, solitary activity where he has been used to a public, social activity (a monologue inside his head versus a dialogue outside him). He must learn to accept that when he reads and writes, and often too, when he listens and speaks, he must conjure up people, places and situations that may be re-created only in the mind.[2] He must accept the fact that his neighbourhood dialect, and the uses to which he puts it, are no longer sufficient in themselves if he is to have a full share of what it means to be literate. He will have new conventions to master, some new grammar to learn (and for *all* native speakers the grammar of the written language is in many ways different from the grammar of spoken language), many new words to acquire – as well as new meanings for familiar words.

It is into such a plan that learning to deal with the orthography fits. It is necessary to master it, but this should not be given undue attention nor should orthographic patterns be isolated from all the other patterns of written language. It was to avoid this happening that, recently, teachers of initial literacy have been urged to ignore spelling mistakes in the child's written work. But, whenever this means that the child is left to discover spelling patterns and all other levels of patterns without some intervention on the teacher's part, it is not wise. The child's needs are not met by ignoring any linguistic patterns, but rather by finding ways of giving appropriate attention to them all.

What do children need to know?

Children as language learners at home

We are now aware that during the first five years of their lives all normal children have almost mastered the spoken language. We also know that to do so they had to master the use of the immensely complex rules of the language. The form of the language they learn is that of their neighbourhood and speakers, in Britain especially, vary greatly in the ways in which they speak.

One 'neighbourhood language' dominates the British speech community: that which we refer to as the Standard Dialect. It has many accents, but only one grammatical form and one standard dictionary. It is not found in any one neighbourhood; it dominates the language of the professions and is found wherever these are practised. When some other neighbourhood languages are compared to it they are frequently said to be inferior, less precise, vulgar, rough. Such opinions are not about *language* but about *people* and *social class*. From a linguistic point of view any neighbourhood language is as capable an instrument of communication as any other.

Children as language learners at school

We do not know how it is that children learn to operate with the rules of their language. Neither they nor any other untrained native speaker knows what these rules are in such a way as to be able to describe them; yet they know how to operate them.

When the child is required to learn a second language medium, that of the written language, he does so after this immense feat of learning to speak and he does so in a very different kind of learning situation. In the one, he was in the highly advantageous position of being able to claim much attention from his family: one child to one or more adults (besides other children). In the school situation, however much teachers are able to give each child individual attention, he is in a learning situation where he is one of 40 or so children to one adult. A simple arithmetical calculation will show how far any teacher may give individual attention to all her children. Out of her available time (when she is free of registers, organisational matters, welfare, assembly and whole-class functions such as singing, story telling) she has less than five minutes for each child each day. It is therefore, not through working with each child individually that she can claim success but rather in the way she is able to make her teaching effective with each individual child. For this to be so, children have to be able to learn *on their own and in groups*. The more understanding they have of what they are doing and the greater their acceptance of the reason for it, the more they will succeed.

In addition to these gross differences between the language learning situation at home and at school, when he learns to become literate, the child is affected by the fact that he is a different learner, in as much as he has largely mastered the spoken language, and by the fact that what he is now learning is not natural to him as his spoken language is. Therefore the written language – embodying as it does a second stage of abstraction from reality–cannot be learned in the same way as spoken language. In learning to speak, the child cannot ask questions about the language he hears around him, for he does not possess the language with which to formulate them. He cannot say 'what was that speech sound?' or 'what does that mean' or 'in which order do I put the words. . .'. When learning to read and write, however easily this is accomplished, he has to ask questions and receive answers. If the answers do not always fit the facts of the language, he has to be able to amend them so that they *do* fit. Children vary in their ability to do this.

To make learning to read and write efficient and economical for the child, he needs some instruction. Through proper instruction he will begin to make discoveries for himself and to gain an awareness of the rules that he has to operate. This *awareness through instruction and discovery* will be enhanced by the extent to which the materials in the classroom reflect the nature of the language and by the way they enable the child to capitalise what he already knows about language in use. *Breakthrough* is an attempt to provide classroom materials of this kind and this book is an attempt to give the teacher the basis on which instruction and discovery procedures may be based. Her attitudes and her ability as teacher and organiser are concerns which are mainly beyond the influence of both. Good teaching will be enhanced by their use.

Methods and Approaches

It is now common to hear of the advocacy of 'mixed methods' in the teaching of reading and the days of the battles between those who believed only in word recognition or in phonics are, we may hope, over. However, to classify the issues involved it is necessary to look at the nature of the written language and at the nature of the learner.

The written language is *visual* and words written with the Roman alphabet are more memorable (because they look different, one from another) than words written in some other alphabetic writing systems (Hebrew, for example). The symbols of the written language, apart from their visual properties also reflect elements of the language. The way it does this is traditionally dealt with by teaching phonics. We have pointed to a major weakness in this area (the orthography does more than relate symbols to sounds), but we agree with those who argue that such knowledge of the nature of the written marks is an essential part of what the child has to learn. However, to begin with, the child has *no* knowledge of this kind and no reason for having it. If we structure his learning so as to provide special sentences, special drills and special practice, we will also remove the possibility of the child using most of his own resources, his own knowledge of the language, his own interests and his need to practise in his own way. The most fortunate children are able to make good the shortcomings of any approach, but not without some delay in reaching the point at which language is used naturally.

Breakthrough to literacy attempts to prevent this delay. We believe that the initial, formal introduction to the written language should be through its visual properties but that, *as soon as possible*, the child should be helped to an awareness of the way in which symbols reflect elements of the language.

This does not imply drills, but rather the piecing together of information from which valid principles will emerge. It is here that the teacher's influence is crucial. The more she knows of the principles underlying the writing system the more able she will be to instruct her children appropriately.

With *Breakthrough* children learn to use the written language in a way that, in some respects at least, is comparable to the way they learned to speak. They compose many written sentences which are never illustrated and which in some cases would be impossible to illustrate.

Because with *Breakthrough* children are able to use

their own linguistic and cultural resources and their own interests, their motives for reading and writing are strong. The dynamic learning situation made possible by the Sentence Maker and the Word Maker, allows for experiment and practice which are not possible in any other way. Children are directly confronted by all the conventions of the writing system and work with them in concrete learning situations.

Using *Breakthrough*, children do much more than memorise written words: they also learn to use words in a variety of grammatical structures. (This fact, and the fact that the words they use are dictated by their own interests, are the chief reasons for their memorability.) Thus appropriate stress is laid on the way children use the grammar to combine words into phrases, clauses and sentences. Word lists are difficult to memorise. Words combined in structures, because they have context, are more easily recalled.

Reading theory, in its most recent past, has been overwhelmingly concerned with words in isolation and with the problems of our orthography. It has taken little note of the way in which all other units of the language at all other levels work. It has attempted a simplification of the language, a task inevitably doomed to failure. *The language cannot be simplified* but our methodology, our approach to teaching and the materials we use can *simplify and clarify the learning situation* so that children are able consciously to acquire knowledge of the orthography, the grammar of written language and the uses to which it may be put – and to become literate.

Bibliography

1 VENEZKY, R. L., 'English orthography: its graphical structure and its relation to sound', *Reading Research Quarterly*, III No. 3, Newark, U.S.A., 1967.

2 MORRIS, R., *Success and Failure in Learning to Read*, p. 72 et seq., Oldbourne, 1965.

8

MORE ABOUT BOOKS

First reading books, *Breakthrough* and others

Breakthrough books

In preparing the 24 *Breakthrough* books we tried to fulfil the following conditions:

1 that the books should be related to the life and interests of the five-year-old, his arrival at school and the impact of this important event on him. Home and school become two interacting circles from which the child views the world. We were concerned to make the texts relevant to the lives and needs of children, of which we took a different view from that of the author of Janet and John, who wrote:

> The themes on which the earlier books are written are the happy carefree incidents which are found in the everyday lives of most children – running with puppy, teaching him to jump, gardening with Mother and Father, paddling, sailing toy boats, buying a toy.[1]

2 that the language of the texts should be related to the linguistic resources of the five-year-old. This meant that at this earliest stage, the written word should represent certain features of children's spoken language; it should use similar sentence structures and cohesive elements while maintaining a sentence length that made appropriate demands on the child's limited reading skill.

3 that sentences should be normal written English sentences: that is they should *look* natural and *sound* natural when read aloud. They should be good models on which the child can build his own resources. This did not preclude the use of an extensive range of sentence types. It meant for example that our texts had to exclude the repetition of words when this was not demanded by the nature of the story or its style.

Most of the *Breakthrough* books are based on conversations with five-year-old children. These 'stories' were written down verbatim and subsequently re-written so as to retain the essential quality of the originals while conforming broadly to the usages of Standard English. In this way we hoped that the result-ing texts would be closely related to the linguistic re-sources of the children, to their interests and to their notions of a 'story'. They are sociologically indetermin-ate in the sense that in them we have attempted to avoid situations or events restricted to one social class. But in another sense they are not so: to the extent that each story attempts to reveal the child's view of his world: they are *children's books*. In them we have depicted situations in which all children find themselves – falling over, dressing up, losing a tooth and going home from school. The books designed to be read first overlap with the texts that we have found children produce when using the Sentence Maker. The child's reading is therefore preceded by work which has made him familiar with almost all the vocabulary items and sentence structures. Because of this it has been possible to exclude from *Breakthrough* books aspects of practice (i.e. repetition of words and sentences in a way that is not demanded by the literary form of the story) that distort the text and give it an unnatural quality. Simi-larly we have not attempted to concentrate on any particular spelling pattern nor on 'high frequency' items.

We make no claim to have discovered the ideal vocabulary for use in early reading books; we believe it does not exist. It is not difficult to visualise another set of books with different lexical items which would be equally satisfactory. In the later books, which are read by the time children are beginning to master our writing system, the subject of each story dictates its own set of lexical items, and the fact that these are in a context to which the child can refer, makes it easy to identify new words. The teacher can help this process by read-ing the story to the children first. She can then discuss new words with them, and may prepare special cards on which these are written, so that children can match cards and words in the text.

From the beginning children need 'information' books
that they can read and use for themselves; books about
the many subjects that interest them. Gardner puts
this well when he writes:

> In a modern infant school there are children with a
> lively interest in subject matter that could be desig-
> nated as physics, mechanics, magnetism, hydro-
> statics, mathematics, engineering, biology and social
> science. It seems rather stupid to feed these young-
> sters with a reading diet of 'see Father with the
> can'.[2]

We have exemplified this in *About the house* and *An
abc for hungry girls and boys*. The first has labelled
illustrations and a simple story; the second presents
sound/symbol correspondences in a novel setting.
There seems no good reason why traditional ABCs
should draw so frequently on wild and domestic animals
for their material rather than on space exploration,
television, sport, science and cooking.

Primers

Some of the most widely used primers are now the
subject of a considerable criticism.[3] They are objected
to because of their content and of the use to which they
are put in the Infants' classroom. Both text and illustrations reflect an unimaginatively stolid middle-class
ethos; the 'adventures' of a happy mummy and a
handsome daddy dealing confidently, if dully, with
smiling children, dog- or cat-attended, in a perpetually
sunlit garden. This is 'real life' for few of our children
and probably wholly uninteresting to all of them
(although, to please their teachers, they accept whatever the teacher recommends – at least for a time). It is
quite possible that a great deal of the assumed common
background of small children – the garden, the pets,
the solicitous parents and the holidays by the sea – is
as strange to many of them as fairyland or outer space.
The children in the slum school in which the authors
worked had little idea of what a garden was. The word
completely baffled one small child until she remembered
that 'garden is a kind of cigarette' (Guard). Another

little girl – an intelligent six-year-old – completed a jig-saw puzzle picture of a man in overalls clipping a high green hedge with a pair of hedge shears. When asked to comment on the completed picture she said rather scornfully, as if it were so patent it didn't need explanation: 'He's drilling the wall with his Black and Decker.' She had interpreted the picture by relating it to the only comparable thing she had seen. These incidents typify the gap between the actual experience of some urban children and the kind of school materials that are offered them. Bruner has commented that:

> . . . a generation ago, the progressive movement urged that knowledge be related to the child's own experience and brought out of the realm of empty abstractions. A good idea was translated into banalities about the home, then the friendly postman and trashman, then the community and so on. It is a poor way to compete with the child's own dramas and mysteries.[4]

The language used in these books is often artificial, and even unique. Forms such as *Dan has a can* or *See the dog. Look, look, look.* are rarely encountered outside the pages of a primer. Books composed entirely from 'high frequency' words are seldom gripping in content, and primers seldom match the language of children or their wide interests. See Appendix 3 for a selection of books.

An introduction to nursery rhymes by Nicholas Tucker

Like fairy tales, most nursery rhymes were never composed with children especially in view. More often, the mother, nursemaid or whoever else, would sing to their child the first thing that came to mind, which is why nursery rhymes have such diverse origins – from bawdy songs to country ballads. Some of these snatches, often after considerable change, gradually became part of the oral tradition, but with none of that deadening over-simplification of ideas and language that tends to run through more self-conscious children's literature.

In fact, the main body of nursery rhymes covers an

enormous range of language and imagination, and with a few regional variations forms a nation-wide link between children everywhere. Their infectious repetitions, rhythms and rhymes are easy to remember at a time when the child may be struggling to master the spoken language, and the vocabulary and grammatical structures he picks up from them can be most useful. Various specific nursery rhymes introduce children to counting, the alphabet, the days of the week and months, the difference between right and left, and on another level bring in the idea that words can be fun to manipulate and play with, in riddles, catches and puzzles. And a child who already knows a rhyme by heart can often come by association to recognise some of the key words of the same rhyme in print, if he sees it often enough in his favourite book.

So far as the imagination is concerned, nursery rhymes are almost unlimited in their appeal to a child. For the baby, there are rhymes and games about parts of his body, while the older child will learn to distinguish sense from nonsense, at a time when he is still naturally confused between fact and fancy, with the aid of such obvious and delightful leg-pulls as *Hey Diddle Diddle, the Cat and the Fiddle*. Other rhymes deal with birth, love and death: topics that are important in a young child's fantasies but which often get ignored in the rest of his literature. The violence that plays such a large part in an Infant's fantasy life is also brought to the surface and put into context by nursery rhymes. Some recent anthologies have become rather shy of these rough, tough old rhymes, just as nineteenth century editors tended to omit the more obviously erotic ones. But a good anthology, with a range of rhymes and illustrations that echoes the range of a child's moods – from tantrums to tenderness – will always keep its fascination for a child. And on another level, the archaic words, strange characters, crazy logic and odd, inconsequential stories will continue, in the words of Walter de la Mare, to 'free the fancy, charm tongue and ear, delight the inward eye,' and as he goes on to say later, offer 'A direct short cut into poetry itself'. See Appendix 4 (p. 195) for a selection of books.

Picture story books

A literacy programme must see its end in the ability of the learner to handle written materials of all kinds and with a multitude of uses, both literary and non-literary. Ideally teachers should attempt to gain some expertise in choosing books for their children, in training the children in the use of libraries and in co-operating with parents to ensure that they understand what the school is attempting to do and how they can best help. Children should read because they want to, for pleasure and the pursuit of knowledge – not because they are compelled to read by class routines or examination requirements. Reading and writing should not be so distasteful to the learner that he will abandon these activities when he is freed from the controlled conditions of the school.

The pedagogic function of books

The books listed in the bibliographies that follow are not only enjoyable and stimulating, providing pleasure and motivation for learning to read and write, they also serve the pedagogic functions dealt with earlier in this manual.

The best of the picture story books, even the ones much too difficult for the children to read themselves, have a strong story line reflected closely in accompanying sequential illustrations. The children may be able to re-tell a story that has become familiar to them by referring to the illustrations and this is one of the very important functions of picture story books. (Bernstein has pointed out the inability of certain children to maintain a subject through continuous discourse.[5]) The frequent use of picture story books for this purpose may well be one of the keys to the development of a range of new speech skills.

Neither the teacher nor the child need be consciously aware of the linguistic knowledge that is imparted during these story sessions. Such is their interest and involvement in the stories that new ideas, new language skills, new aspects of grammar and new items of vocabulary are learned without conscious effort. The telling and reading of stories is a vital part of English teaching for all Infants' School children, especially for those who do not have this experience at home. Thus the way in which parts of a text hang together, becomes available to the child through the reading and telling and discussion of stories.

More obviously there will be vocabulary extensions as the child encounters new words. For instance, many five-year-olds do not understand the family relationship specified in such words as uncle, nor are they necessarily familiar with the hierarchy common to fairy stories. The child is not only learning the meaning of the special relationships involved, he is sorting out concepts of family and social life.

Picture story books

The lists of picture story books in Appendix 5 are intended to be representative rather than comprehensive. We have set out some of the books we have found successful with five- and six-year-olds. Though the books listed here are very simple, it is not important to be too concerned about the level of difficulty of stories read or told to very young children. As Ehrenzweig has said:

> Children can listen breathlessly to a tale of which they understand only a little. In the words of William James they take 'flying leaps' over long stretches that elude their understanding and fasten on the few points that appeal to them. This ability of understanding – and it is an ability – may be due to their . . . capacity to comprehend the total structure rather than analysing single elements.[6]

The bibliography was originally compiled and annotated by Mrs Griselda Barton and has been revised by Brian Thompson.

See Appendix 5 (p. 197) for a selection of books.

Bibliography

1 MUNRO, R., *Janet and John Teacher's Manual*, Nesbit, 1954.
2 GARDNER, KEITH, in *Reading* 1, No. 3, December 1967.
3 *Children and Their Primary Schools*, paragraph 587. op. cit.
4 BRUNER, JEROME S., *Towards a theory of instruction*, Harvard University Press, 1966.
5 BERNSTEIN, BASIL, 'Elaborated and Restricted Codes', *American Anthropologist* special issue: 'Ethnography of Speech'. December 1964.
6 EHRENZWEIG, ANTON, *The Hidden Order of Art*. London, Weidenfeld and Nicolson, 1967.

9

WORK WITH *BREAKTHROUGH TO LITERACY* IN THE REMEDIAL SITUATION

In discussing the work of the normal Infant School child we have referred to the shortage of time and the importance attached to literacy in contemporary society. The child who enters the Junior School unable to read and write, perhaps because he has spent the minimum time in the Infant School, is already in a remedial situation. Every term that passes before the initial step into literacy has been taken, makes his position more serious. The children around him use their literacy skills successfully for their whole education, while he falls further and further behind them. To protect himself, he may begin to develop the defensive attitudes familiar to teachers who work with such children.

Every remedial teacher knows that she is not dealing with an easily defined problem. The individuals she has to teach may well have a wide variety of problems concerned with their physical and mental health, and chronic or sudden home difficulties. Many of these children, especially the older ones and those in special schools, are in need of help from specialist services. The majority also need to make good deficiencies in their cultural backgrounds by listening to the reading and telling of stories, by making out-of-school visits, by discussions with adults, by making things, painting, listening to music, looking after pets – all the things which the best schools provide. We would not for a moment suggest that *Breakthrough* replaces any of the specialist advice which a remedial child may need or that it makes up for lack of cultural enrichment. We do say that the *Breakthrough* materials can help any individual child to overcome the difficulty of starting to read and write, and that they are flexible in use so that each child can work individually.

Although the materials have been designed for the use of Infant children in the normal school situation, two of the key items – the Sentence Maker and the Word Maker – are of considerable help to slow learners. They can be used with children of any age, including those at Secondary level, to enable these children to compose their own texts and read them back. The books accompanying the project materials and also the Nursery Rhyme cards and record have been used with benefit and pleasure with older children but their relevance to the situation must be assessed by the teacher. It is difficult to be specific about the benefits which result from the use of these other materials in situations which may range from the near-adult to the first year Junior School child, from the child of very low I.Q. in a Training Centre to the highly intelligent child who has some specific difficulty with literacy. About the Sentence Maker and the Word Maker there need be no reservations.

Two of the great difficulties facing the remedial teacher are the shortage of suitable reading material and the fact that once work has started, words which were recognised by a child one day, seem to be forgotten the next day. Thus, for many children, little progress is made.

The details of the processes by which we learn to recognise and use written words are not fully understood, but when children are able to handle word cards and move them about, using them in many different contexts while they are doing so, they learn these words and remember them. The children with whom we have worked were able to read texts they had composed after a four-week holiday. They were able to recognise their own vocabulary items so that they would say immediately 'This is not my word' if one was put in their Sentence Maker by mistake. It is as well to check through the personal words of a child fairly often, for, as they will ask for words which they may only use once or twice, these will be less securely known. But if one of these less used words is forgotten in a spot check, draw the attention of the child to the sentence in which it was used and, almost invariably, it will be remembered. Later, when the child is reading texts other than his own, if a familiar word is not recognised in its printed form, reference back to that word in his own sentence will help him to recognise it. It is the involvement in a self-made text which is the heart of this learning process.

The practice element of this learning, referred to in work with five-year-old children, is often very evident in the work of the slower child also. The following are examples made by a girl of nearly twelve when she started to use the Sentence Maker, and it is typical of the work of many such children:

I go to school with my mum.
I go to school with my friend.
I go to school with my story.
I go to school with my book.
I go to school with my brother.
I run to school with my brother.
I walk to school with my brother.
I skip to school with my brother.

Sentence making of this type is not in any sense a waste of time nor is it the result of laziness, nor of an inability to make other sentence patterns. Children who do this are often those who will soon make a noticeable step forward into many different kinds of sentences and become the first to write sentences without making them in the Stand. Perhaps they only needed the opportunity to practise and reinforce some written patterns of the language so that they could continue confidently. These sentences closely resemble the sort of spoken sentences practised by babies when they are learning to speak. For some children written practice of the same type may be essential to their future success.

One aspect of literacy learning is usually accentuated in the remedial situation: teachers very often refer only to remedial reading groups (and parents are anxious that their child should at least be able to read a little). The children themselves are presented for a very long period with other people's texts. Writing is often taught by asking the child to fill in blanks in other people's sentences, from a list of words supplied. Yet experience shows that these are the very children who find the greatest difficulty in learning in this way. They are the very ones who need a great deal of opportunity for production (composition of texts) in place of the struggle with the reception (reading) of special primer texts.

With *Breakthrough* materials the child produces his own reading material and quite soon he may also show interest in the work of other children. This is nearly always easier to read than the texts in books. Such sentences are constructed in ways that are natural to children of the same age and embody common interests and experiences.

With the use of the Sentence Maker children will compose texts of varied content – from fairy stories to facts about home and school; from a long story about 'The Crocodile in my Bath' by a twelve-year-old girl to the stark little statement of a child waiting for transfer to an E.S.N. school: 'I will not think about what I cannot do.' There need be no limit placed on the kinds of texts produced. The first result of using Sentence Makers with the older children is often a notable improvement in the amount and quality of their written work. Instead of filling in gaps in pre-arranged texts the child has now to grapple with the composition of complete sentences. It is also the opportunity for the teacher to discuss with the child any mistakes that have been made in a sentence – if it is incompletely made, if the tense is wrongly constructed, if there is an error in word recognition. All such occasions are opportunities for teaching and talking about aspects of the English language, and this discussion is a most important part of the learning situation.

When the wrong word has been used by mistake, this is time to begin the use of the Word Maker. Teachers in Special Schools will judge for themselves to what degree the Word Maker can profitably be used, but with children in remedial groups in the ordinary schools it is a great help. It should be used in exactly the same way as with Infant children. As is the case with the Sentence Maker the Word Maker allows for the physical handling of the symbols and this makes a far deeper and more lasting impact on the child than the attempt to write the word (with subsequent crossing and rubbing out). Certainly it has far greater impact than copying down someone else's spelling and attempting to 'learn' it; a procedure which for most of these children has met with little success in the past.

The Junior School

Ideally the slower child should enter the Junior School from an Infant department where *Breakthrough* materials are in use. He should bring his Sentence Maker and a Word Maker with him, and at the appropriate time, abandon these materials just as the faster child abandoned them in the Infant department. However unfamiliar the materials are to Junior class teachers they are likely to appreciate the fact that the slow child can continue to work confidently. Without the materials it is necessary for the teacher to find another approach for children who have not yet made a start. In some areas, of course, no slow or remedial children will pass from the Infant School and teachers in these schools will have no interest in the *remedial* uses of the materials. However, each year many Junior Schools receive a number of children either with no reading age (on a word or sentence test) or a reading age below six. There may be many reasons for this – the district in which the school is situated, unavoidable staff changes in the Infant School, a number of 'problem' children passing to the Juniors at the same time, size of classes. We have suggested that some of these difficulties may need specialist attention. The *Breakthrough* materials will enable the children to concentrate on their first practical step into literacy.

In Junior Schools the usual practice is for a remedial teacher to have groups of children (the smaller the better) for some time each day. If the children concerned can take their Sentence Makers back to the classroom and use them there after their group time, this is ideal, but this is a decision for both the class teacher and the remedial teacher to make. One practical difficulty in this situation is the acquisition of new words; the materials will probably be kept wherever the remedial teacher works and this may mean that children have to go to her to get new words. What happens may depend on how many children are involved and for how much of the day the remedial teacher is present.

In most cases the work is likely to be limited to the remedial group period and it is recommended that this time be taken up initially with as much sentence making as possible and with writing these down and reading them back.

By the time they reach the Junior School, almost all children (including those with no reading age) know a number of words to be found in the Sentence Maker. Each child can, therefore, start work with his own Sentence Maker. At first the teacher should have each child on his own and should go through the words it contains with him, making a small pencil dot under each word he recognises. Then she should help him to place the inserts in the appropriate pockets.

He may not be able to make a simple sentence with the words he has first recognised – for instance they may be *mum, school, baby, little, the, a, and*. In this case he should start by making phrases like 'mum and a baby' to enable him to see how the materials are used. Where a child recognises a number of words, sentence work can flourish from the beginning. If the school is in a deprived area and a group of children enter the Junior department knowing no words at all, it may be necessary to start with the teacher's materials and the Magnet Board, exactly as with Infants. In schools where *Breakthrough* materials have been tried with Junior remedial groups, although all the children were able to make some start with individual Sentence Makers, it has also been found that work with the Magnet Board is a great help in encouraging children to experiment with new words and new ideas.

Junior children who meet these materials for the first time are helped by the fact that these are quite different from the books which they already associate with failure. They will have some immediate success no matter how small it may be. Every sentence or near sentence made will be the occasion for praise and encouragement, and the child will very soon become involved in the work. Even the child (well known to every remedial teacher) who seems to have no ability to concentrate, will be intrigued long enough to make one or two sentences and, with patient encouragement, this span will gradually increase – especially as sentence making of this kind involves him in playing an active and creative part.

Many of the children will be able to write their own sentence into their books. If they have difficulty with handwriting, however, the teacher should write it for them. She should then teach handwriting separately. In any case it is necessary to check that they have written legibly and that they have copied down each sentence correctly. It is important that they should always have a good model to read from.

Each time the child comes for his lesson let him read many of the sentences that he has written before. Suggest that any new words acquired the day before be used to make his new sentences. With children who find the work difficult the slow steady progress is essential. Occasionally there will also be the child who is suddenly released by working with a Sentence Maker and who is able to rush ahead.

Children should learn to use the full stop and the question mark from the beginning. They may also be anxious to use capital letters and speech marks (many will have heard of these) and it is easy for the teacher to make them on blank card. Their use can be discussed fully so that children understand this. The discussion and explanation of these conventions help the child to use them correctly in the Sentence Maker, where the fear of making mistakes is removed because of the way in which the cards can be moved into alternative positions. When he comes to write his sentences down, the learning is reinforced.

Because he has correct spelling patterns before him, the slower child may improve in his ability to spell for himself. At the same time he will probably need a great deal of practice in using the Word Maker as well. Any games which teach and reinforce regular spelling patterns should be tried. Some have already been suggested for the Infant School children.

Each child should, at first, use his own sentences as his first reading material. In the course of the work all the children should read each other's sentences and discuss them together. Special books of some of these sentences (including the most interesting and the most varied) should be made for the group, and when the making of books has been established, all the children should be encouraged to contribute sentences which can be put together into a continuous story. Such books are usually read with great enthusiasm.

Some of the 24 *Breakthrough* books, may be suitable for these older children: *People in stories, My story* and *In Bed*, for instance, would all be quite suitable for young, slow juniors. Some others may not seem to be suitable but in practice children have been found to enjoy them in spite of the fact that they were written for younger children. The subject matter does not worry them when they find the language used is similar to their own. They may also have another reason for liking a book: one remedial Secondary girl said of *things I can do*, which is aimed very definitely at the interest of Infants' School children, 'I like this book'. When asked why she liked it she replied, surprised by the question, 'Because I can read it.' She may also have meant that the book measured up to her expectations of what books, and the language of books, should be like.

As in all learning processes, fast progress in working with the Sentence Maker may be followed by a period of consolidation and apparent stand-still. When such a point has been reached, the teacher should not try to hurry children away from the work. Sometimes children who have started to write quite freely, without first making the sentences in the stand, revert to simple sentence making for a time. Any slow child should be allowed to use the Sentence Maker for as long as he wishes. Even when he does not need to build up the sentences first, he may still find it helpful to have his word store to refer to, to make sure of spellings and constructions.

The Secondary School

The number of illiterate children entering the Secondary Schools is comparatively small, but for them the problem is severe. Having failed consistently for six years of their lives leaves a mark on their personalities, quite apart from the educational loss it represents. Remedial teachers will be familiar with the symptoms these children show — ranging from the hardened 'If I can't do it it's not worth doing' outlook to the blushing, sweating nervousness of the child who is still trying desperately despite his conviction of failure. Sentence work is not just a form of therapy but it *can* provide what may be the child's last chance of entering the world of the written word.

A small experimental group of Secondary School children has used the *Breakthrough* materials and the results have been encouraging. Work with the Sentence Makers was found to follow the same course with these children as with those in the Junior remedial groups. Secondary children who are illiterate are usually given extra help in small groups.

The same pattern of development shows itself with children of this age as with slow Junior and some Infant children. At first imperfect sentences are made and read back as though perfect. Later, short sentences are practised in much the same way as with the younger children. The older children go on doing this until they have gained confidence, and often follow such practice by a sudden burst of progress. The following is an example of the way the work of one child developed: September, 1968. She made these sentences in her Stand:

I like to run and play.
I like to play with my friend.
some teachers are horrible.
some girls are horrible.
some boys are horrible.
I am not horrible.
I am a good girl.

May, 1969. Written without making the sentences in her Stand:

One day was a witch who live in a old house and three was gold shoes in the princess garden and the witch wanted the gold shoe but the princess didn't give her the gold shoe. the princess wanted to give the gold shoe to a little girl the witch didn't like the little girl but the princess didn't care. The little girl was frightened of the witch the next day the princess give the little girl the gold shoe. In the end the little girl was going home and the witch take the little girl away.

(aged 12)

This girl could only draw a picture and label it with one word from a given list of words when she first came to the Secondary School. After she had graduated from the Sentence Maker she was able to write stories using it only as a reminder of her earlier work with it. Occasionally she had queries about spelling.

Working with the Sentence Maker with these children brought to light points at which they had become enmeshed in difficulties and completely blocked by them. It is often said that the writing of a remedial child is nonsense; but very often, this 'nonsense' was found to be similar to the first sentences made by Infants' children – grammatical parts of the sentence omitted and the importance of word order not yet fully understood in the written medium. The possibility of moving words around and of discussing their order was found to be of the greatest importance in furthering children's understanding of what they were doing. The more everything was discussed the greater the progress they made.

The sentences they composed were made to look more like adult reading matter and closer to the printed word, by being typed on loose-leaf paper. They then had a book in which they wrote the sentences they had just made in the stands, as well as a file with a typed version of the same sentences. (It may be argued that the Secondary child could type his own sentences but, apart from the shortage of typewriters, this is a slow process which causes them to become impatient and leads them to make many mistakes. At this stage the aim is to jump the child over the hurdle of initial literacy – not to involve him in typing lessons.) The file of typed sentences was very useful in helping him to produce some written work in other contexts. After a short time it included a wide range of English sentence patterns and these were adapted for use in subject lessons as though they were items in a foreign language phrase book. Among their own sentences the children found the useful phrase, the correct spelling of a word they wished to use, and wrote with regained confidence.

The written and typed sentences were the first reading material for the Secondary child. Again this was broadened to include the reading of sentences composed by all the children in the group. In addition typed copies of a variety of new and interesting sentences were circulated among them. Each child found his own sentences easy to read and the sentences of other children only a little more difficult. Children of this age soon appreciated the possibility of collecting together and ordering sentences to make simple stories. These stories, in a typed form, became the first group-books. The children chose not to illustrate them (they could have done so had they wished); they no longer needed additional visual clues to be able to read extensively from typed stories they had themselves written. With the confidence gained in this work the children's writing became fluent, although it was often messy in its handwritten version and there were still mistakes in detail.

The transition to printed books was difficult for children of this age because so few of the available books were simple enough and relevant to their interests. Some of them read the Breakthrough books quite happily after they were told plainly 'These books were written for much younger children than you. Have a look at them and see what you think about them.' Their opinions and comments were taken seriously. No one had spent longer looking at Infants' reading books than they had; they were not likely to accept any they did not like. In this critical frame of mind most of the children in the group read the Breakthrough books quite happily and with undisguised relief at achieving success at last. Some of the children also used the books as a source for words needed in their writing (for example *People in stories* for fairy stories and *The Christmas tree* for seasonal writing).

Once sentence making was well established the Word Maker became very important. It was also used with groups of children who were already reading and writing to a fairly adequate standard but who still had difficulty with spelling. Some of them arrived at their Secondary School not only with no idea about regular spelling patterns but with the additional burden of ingrained misspellings. Handling the symbol cards and rearranging them until a word appeared in its correct spelling increased the confidence of these children. With a pencil on paper the old faults seemed inevitable; the pencil seemed to lead the hand into well learned mistakes whereas the arrangement of the symbols in a stand gave word making a 'new look'.

All the work with the Word Maker suggested for Infants should be taken with the Secondary child at this stage. Some of the more complex patterns should be practised as well. For instance, a group might make the word *fight* and then change the first symbol to make as many words as possible. They might agree about *light, might, night, right, sight, tight*; but *bight, dight* and *wight* might lead to further discussion and to the further possibility of making *chight* or *gight*. The section on spelling rules in Appendix I of this manual will help the teacher to the full use of the Word Maker.

The School for the Educationally Sub-normal Child

No member of the team has any qualification or special training for dealing with sub-normal children nor had we such children in mind when the *Breakthrough* materials were designed. Nevertheless we were very pleased that one E.S.N. school joined our project for the experimental year. We explained the materials and their use to the staff concerned and left them to use the materials in the way they thought best.

They have worked very much in the way an Infants' teacher would, but with children who are slightly older. The Magnet Board was found to be very helpful for starting both discussion and sentence work. In this school too, attention has been concentrated on sentence work and it has developed well. Near the end of the first term we made for each child who had started composing sentences independently, a book with one sentence typed on each page. The child took this book home to read to his parents and to illustrate during the holidays. This evidence of progress encouraged both the parents and the child.

No child had any difficulty in handling and arranging the Sentence Maker words, but some children have made more progress than others. The teachers' impressions of the results of this work were that each child had progressed further with *Breakthrough* materials than with any others they had tried previously, that the children had become very much involved in the work and had greatly enjoyed it.

The Training Centre

The children in the Training Centre, because of the severity of handicaps from which they suffer, present a most difficult educational problem and one which we would not have ventured to consider had not the Centre concerned requested to experiment with *Breakthrough*. Originally the staff thought that only the Teacher's Sentence Maker would be of any use to their children. However, a group of the most able children are now using individual Sentence Makers with success. They are also reading several of the books. The enjoyment which these children get from their work is very moving and the success they have achieved surprising. Most of them were not expected to be able to take any steps towards literacy and, indeed, if they had found it too difficult or in any way upsetting, it would have been most unfair to have expected them to do so. However, they show the greatest delight in the work and there is every evidence that they understand what they are doing. They read with meaning and they are able to link words and sentences in *Breakthrough* books to the appropriate pictures.

APPENDICES

APPENDIX I

SOME NOTES ON ENGLISH SPELLING

1 Consonant symbols

In presenting the following information about symbols and the elements of the language they represent, examples are restricted to words likely to be used by primary school children. They provide a wide range of spelling patterns (although not the complete range) and from these the basic principles of English spelling emerge.

Note: The spelling of words like *home, here, how, his* is likely to be difficult for children who do not have the *aspirate h*, and who say *'ome, 'ere, 'ow, 'is.*

Such children need help which comes best from the teacher who is aware of variations in the normal speech habits of the English speaking community.

Consonant symbols which regularly represent one speech sound

b, bb regularly correspond to sound b in **big** and **bubble**.

b corresponds to *no speech sound* in lamb, bomb; (but note bombard).

f regularly corresponds to sound f in **father, five, fall**.

f corresponds to sound v in of (the only exception to the above).

h represents the voiceless air stream to be found at the beginning of words like **ha, hot, harmony**. As a consonant symbol it is found in initial position in a syllable, except in exclamations like **ah, oh, hurrah**, where it signals the representation of the length of the previous vowel sound and not a speech sound after that vowel sound.

h regularly represents the h sound in **hospital**.

It represents *no speech sound* in vehicle, honest, honour, hour.

j regularly corresponds to the soft g sound in **joy, jack**. It is found only in initial syllable position in words (except for a foreign borrowing like **raj**).

k regularly corresponds to the k sound in **kick, king, keep, kangaroo**.

k represents no sound when followed by n initially in the following words: **knack, knap-sack, knave, knead, knee,**

knell, knick, knife, knight, knit, knob, knock, knoll, knot, know, knowledge, knuckle.

l, ll represents the l sounds in **play, health, apple, lip, hill.** (For notes on words like *fall, halt, bald, talk, half,* see p. 171 on vowels *a* and *o*.)

m, mm regularly represents the sound in **my, mummy.**

n, nn regularly represents the sound in **not, funny.**

p, pp regularly represents the sound in **pin, poppy.**
p represents no sound in present day pronunciation of words like **corps, receipt** and in words beginning **pn, ps, pt.**
ph regularly corresponds to the f sound in **photo, elephant.**

r, rr followed by a vowel, regularly represents the sound in **red, furry.**
r preceded by vowels – see note on p. 171.

sh regularly represents the sound in **shop, fish.**

t, tt represents the t sounds in **ten, attend.**
t represents no sound in the following words: **mortgage, buffet, valet, chalet.**
th regularly represents the voiceless sound in **thing, bath.**
th regularly represents the voiced sound in **this, them, that, rather.**
-the regularly represents the voiced sound in **clothe, bathe.**
(*Note:* **th** represents t in words like **Thames, Thomas**)

u occasionally represents the w sound as in **language, anguish.**
u is also associated with q, (q is never found on its own in English words).

q regularly represents the k sound in **queen, antique.**

v regularly represents the sound in **van, anvil.**
When it would otherwise be the last letter written in a word it is always followed by letter **e.**
Thus **ve** is the only way of ending a written word which represents a spoken word with a final v sound. For example: **have, give, live, above.**
In certain recent contractions a final **e** is not written following **v**, for example: **lav, spiv, rev.**

w is both a consonant symbol and part of complex vowel symbols.
w regularly represents the lip-rounded sound in **wool, wife.**
wh no longer represents in Southern English speech the aspirated sound to be found in Scots accents. Thus symbols **w** and **wh** are pronounced identically (for example compare **which** and **witch; when** and **went**). For Scots speakers the

words in these groups sound different and their spellings are not confused.

wr is used initially in a small number of words, and may be regarded as another way of writing symbol **r**.
Note particularly **wr**ap, **wr**en, **wr**ite, **wr**ote, **wr**ung.

w + a produces a set of spelling patterns involving a small number of words, together representing the short and long sounds in **want** and **war**. These patterns do not include words such as *wax*. (See page 168.)

x regularly represents sounds **k** and **s**. It is found in the final position in a syllable. Its use avoids the need for a final letter **s** which is most frequently associated with (1) plurality and (2) 3rd person singular present tense. Compare *lax*, and *lacks*; *wax*, and *whacks*.

y is both a consonant symbol and a vowel symbol. It is more frequently used as a vowel symbol.

y as a consonant symbol regularly represents the initial sound in **yes**, **yellow**.

z, **zz** regularly the voiced sound heard at the beginning of **zoo**, **zig**, **zag** and also in words like **maze**, **razor**, **prize**. When the **z** sound occurs finally in a syllable or word it is frequently represented by the following symbols (1) **s** as in i**s**, boy**s**, flie**s**, also mi**s**er (2) **se** as in rai**se**, ea**se**.
But note **-se** preceded by a **vowel** and **r** as in **horse**, **Morse**, does not represent the **z** sound.

Consonant symbols which represent more than one speech sound

c represents two sounds. The choice between these is signalled by means of the symbol which follows.

c regularly represents the hard **k** sound in the following circumstances:

    c + a, as in *cat*.
    c + o as in *cot*.
    c + u as in *cut*.
    c + a consonant as in *clip*, *clop*.
    c + oo as in *cool*.
    c + oa as in *coat*.
    c final as in *music*.

c regularly represents the soft **s** sound in the following circumstances:

    c + i, as in *city*, *acid*
    c + e, as in *cent*, *ace*

(Note exceptions in **c** in **cello** and **concerto**.)
ch represents three sounds.

ch represents the **tsh** sound in a majority of words with this symbol: as in **church, chop.**

ch represents the hard **k** sound in words beginning **chl-** and **chr-**: **chlorine, chloroform, Christmas, chronometer, chronic, chrysanthemum, chrysalis** and in the following (which are the commonest words of this kind): *ache, choir, lichen, stomach, character, chord, mechanic, chasm, chorus, orchestra, chemist, echo, orchid.*

ch represents the **sh** sound in the following words: **chalet, chauffeur, chiffon, machine, champagne, charade, chef, chivalry, moustache, chandelier, chassis, chevron, chute, crochet.**

s, ss, regularly represents the **s** sound in **sit, miss;** the **z** sound in **as, daisy.**

s represents the **sh** sound in **sure, sugar.**

In the following words **s** represents no sound: **aisle, corps, island, isle chassis, debris.**

g corresponds to the soft **g** sound in *gem,* before **e, i, y,** – as in *gem, gin, gyrate* –

except for: anger, giddy, girder, monger, begin, gift, girdle, target, eager, gig, girl, tiger, finger, giggle, girth, together, forget, gild, give, yogi, gear, gill, hunger, get, gilt, linger (and a few other rarer words).

g, gg, corresponds to the hard **g** sound in all other words e.g.: **grass, goose, game, glide, guide, luggage.**

The confusion of overlap between these two correspondences is therefore limited to the list above.

g preceded by **n** corresponds to the final sound in **sing** except in the comparative (longer) and superlative (longest) in which the **ing** sound and the hard **g** sound are represented by **ng.** Note that in a word like **singer** in which the suffix is not the comparative adjective, the hard **g** sound is not found in southern English speech. It is, however, to be heard in the speech of certain Midlands accents.

g preceded by **i** corresponds to no speech sound and must be taken as part of the complex vowel symbol **ig.** The effect of this **g** symbol is to signal the long **i** vowel correspondence in single syllable words (compare **sin, sign.** But in **signal** the symbols are **s, i, g, = sig** and **nal = nl**) where the syllable boundary falls between **g** and **n** the **i** symbol corresponds to the short **i** and the **g** corresponds to the hard **g.** In **sign** the vowel symbol is **ig** – one of the instances in which a traditional consonant letter becomes part of a vowel cluster.

-gh (final) corresponds to the **f** sound in the following words: **cough, draught, enough, laugh, rough, tough, trough.**

gh (initial) corresponds to the hard g sound in the following: **gh**astly, **gh**ost, spa**gh**etti. (See **h** as marker p. 179.)
gh is part of the complex vowel symbol **ough, augh** in th**ough**, thr**ough** b**ough**, pl**ough**, t**augh**t.
The group of words involving **au** or **ou** + **gh** is very small. The above are the most important of these.

Consonant and vowel symbols representing the sh, zh sound

si regularly represents the zh sound in fu**si**on.
ssi regularly represent the sh sound in mi**ssi**on.
ti regularly represent the sh sound in na**ti**on, ra**ti**on.

Special doubled forms

Most of our consonant symbols have a doubled form, for example: **bb** in bu**bb**le. However, **ph, gh, sh, wh** are never doubled. Certain other consonants are doubled in a way which does not make this completely obvious:

the doubled form of **c**, or **k** is **ck** as in ba**ck**, lo**ck**.
the doubled form of **ch** is **tch** as in ma**tch**, hu**tch**.
the doubled form of **ge** is **dge** as in he**dge**.
(Compare **dge** in he**dge** with **ge** in ra**ge**.)

2 Vowel symbols

The simple vowel symbols

The letters a, e, i, o, u, as written symbols, represent both the short vowel sound and the long vowel sound, according to certain rules.

I When the vowel symbol is followed by two consonant symbols or by a doubled consonant, *it always represents the short vowel*. For example:

in monosyllables

	with two consonants following the vowel symbol	with doubled consonants ck, ff, ll, ss, zz, tch, dge	no initial consonant
a	and	back, batch, badge	add
e	bend	beck, Bess, bell	egg, err, ebb
i	mint	bill, miss, fizz	inn
o	font	boss, moss, dodge	odd
u	fund	buzz, fuss, stuff	

2 When syllables of structure CVC are followed by a second syllable with an initial vowel or **-le**, the structure becomes CVCC + second syllable. For example, when **-ing, -ies, -ed, -en, -er, -est, -y, -le** make the second syllable:

	a	e	i	o	u
-ing	batting	betting	fitting	trotting	humming
-ies	patties	pennies	hippies	follies	bullies
-ed	batted	penned	ribbed	robbed	rubbed
-en	fatten	batten	bitten	rotten	stricken
-er	hatter	setter	tipper	topper	rubber
-est	fattest	reddest	thinnest	hottest	dullest
-y	fatty	telly	ditty	knotty	nutty
-le	battle	kettle	little	throttle	bubble

3 In monosyllables of structure CVC, the vowel symbol represents a short vowel sound. Before the addition of a suffix, the final consonant is repeated (i.e. doubled).

4 In monosyllables of structure CVC + e, the vowel symbol represents a long vowel except for a small group of words ending in **-me, -ne, -ve**, listed below. This **e** we refer to as *the e marker*.[1] Before the addition of all suffixes except **-ly, -lier, -liest** and **-ful** the final **-e** is deleted, as it is no longer needed to provide a contrast with the single consonant of CVC words.

	syllable CVC	syllable CVC + suffix		syllable CVCe	CVC + suffix
	single consonant	double consonant		single consonant + e	single consonant only
short a	mat	matting	long a	mate	mating
e	met	mettle	e	mete	meter
i	bit	bitten	i	bite	biting
o	hop	hopped	o	hope	hoping
u	cut	cutter	u	cute	cutest

5 A few words ending in **-me**, **-ne**, **-se**, **-ve** do not follow this pattern.
For example:

	-me	-ne	-se	-ve
short a				have
short i				give
o = short u	come*	done*		love*
	some*	none*		shove*
				above*
				dove*
				glove*
o = long oo			lose	move*
			whose	prove*
o = short o		gone		
		shone		

*Note: The letter **o** is an alternative to letter **u** in certain circumstances. This is because in handwritten manuscripts confusion was once caused when letter **u** occurred adjacent to letters made of upright strokes. As **u** is also composed of uprights, a multiplicity of these strokes, especially at a time when no dot was written over **i**, rendered the reading extremely ambiguous and difficult. Letter **o** was written instead of **u** to avoid this. Note also the following words in which this use of letter **o** is to be found: *won, wonder, worry, woman, monk, monkey, sponge, ton, tongue, honey, cover, above, lover, comfort, word, mother, plover, front.*

6 In monosyllables with simple vowel symbols which are final, these represent the long vowel sound. *All words of this kind are grammatical words.*

long a – in a (with strong stress: *I* asked for *a* book).
long e – in me, he, she, we, be, the.*
long i – in I.
long i – in thy, my, by, why.
long o – in go, so, no.
long oo – in do, who.

* (the last with strong stress, or when a vowel follows. Compare: The milkman's here. The other day he came later than this. He's the best milkman.)

Simple vowel symbols with r, l, w and wh, and with f, th, s[2]

1 With r

The letters **a, e, i, o, u**, combine with **r** to form symbols representing the long **a** (father) the long neutral vowel — the long schwa (her) and the **aw** sound (for). In spoken words of this kind which are followed by a vowel, the **r** sound is heard — for example 'I met her and her mother' where, in the first occurrence of her, the **r** may be heard.

the long a   **-ar** in car, star.
the long schwa **-er** in her.
the long schwa **-ir** in bird, fir, stir.
the long aw   **-or** in for, fork.
the long schwa **-ur** in fur.

Where a suffix is added, as in the previous section, the **r** is doubled. For example: *star, starry; fur, furry.*

The letters **e, o** combine with **r** to form symbols representing the short schwa in syllables with weak stress. For example:

-er in mother, tiger.
-or in doctor, actor.

The letters **a, e, i, o, u**, combine with **r** and the **e** marker to form symbols representing diphthongs. For example:

-are in care, dare
-ere in mere
-ire in fire, tyre
-ore in core, more
-ure in sure, lure
-ure in pure, cure

2 With l

The letters **a** and **o** combine with **-ll** and **-lt, -ld, -lk, -lf, -lr** to represent the long **aw** (hall), the long **a** (father) and tl long **o** (home). For example:

the long aw – **a + ll** in hall   the long o – **o + ll** in toll
                a + lt in halt   **o + lt** in bolt
                a + ld in bald   **o + ld** in old
no l sound in spoken words   no l sound in spoken words
                a + lk in talk   **o + lk** in folk
the long a   **–a + lm** in alm   **o + lm** in holm
                a + lf in half

3 With f, th, s

The letters **a** and **o** combine with **ff, ft, th, ss, sp, st, sk** to represent the long **a** sound (father) and the long **o** sound (home). For example:

the long a — a + **ff** in cha**ff**
      a + **ft** in **aft**
      a + **th** in p**ath**   the long o — o + **th** in b**oth**
      a + **ss** in p**ass**
      a + **sp** in r**asp**
      a + **st** in m**ast**   the long o — o + **st** in m**ost**
      a + **sk** in m**ask**

4 With w, wh and qu (wa-, wha-, qua-)

The letter **a** combines with **w**, and with **u** in symbol **qu-** to represent the short **o** sound (h**o**t) and the long **aw** sound (h**a**ll). For example:

the short **o** sound — w + **a** in **wa**d, **wa**ddle, **wa**ft, **wa**llet, **wa**n, **wa**nder, **wa**nt, **wa**rrant, **wa**rren, **wa**rrior, **wa**s, **wa**sh, **wa**sp, **wa**tch, **wa**tt, **wa**ttle.

the long **aw** sound — w + **a** in **wa**ltz, **wa**lrus, **wa**lnut.

the short **o** sound — **wh** + **a** in **wha**t.

               qu + **a** in s**qua**sh, s**qua**t, s**qua**d, s**qua**bble, s**qua**nder, s**qua**lor.

the long **aw** sound — w + **ar** in **war**, **war**ble, **war**d, **war**den, **war**m, **war**n, **war**p.

               wh + **ar** in **whar**f.

Symbol o and the chief sounds it represents:

regular long o	long o	regular short o	short u	short or long oo
bone	both	moth	mother	woman
go	most	broth	other	who
	ghost	froth	plover	whose
	post	lost	money	whom
	host	cost	honey	move
			monk	prove
			none	do
			done	
			glove	
			shove	
			love	
			above	
			dove	
			oven	

The Complex vowel symbols

The letters **a, e, i, o, u,** combine with one another and with **y, w, r, g, gh, h,** to form a further set of complex vowel symbols. Some of these are rare.

	a	e	i/y	o	u/w	r	g/gh h
a	**aa** baa	**ae** Aesop	**ai** maid **ay** may	—	**au** laud **aw** law	**ar** car	— **ah**
e	**ea** sea head	**ee** see	**ei** receive **ey** key grey	**eo** people	**eu** Europe **ew** new	**er** her	— **eh**
i	**ia** Ian	**ie** lie **ye** bye	—	—	—	**ir** girl	**ig,** **igh** sign high
o	**oa** boat	**oe** canoe	**oi** boil **oy** boy	**oo** (short) book (long) food	**ou** out **ow** snow cow	**or** for doctor	— —
u	—	**ue** blue	**ui** build **uy** buy	—	—	**ur** fur	— —

In the above chart the letters i, y, and the letters u, w, are grouped together in the top line. The following notes set out to explain the reason for this:

the letters **i**, and **u** are not written finally in words other than foreign borrowings: when this would otherwise occur **y** is used to replace **i**, and **w** to replace **u**. In addition an e marker is added in some words so that i and u are not final (for example, **blue** and **lie**, *not* blu, li). Thus we have **laid** but not **lai** (which is written **lay**) **toil** but not **toi** (which is written **toy**) **cause** but not **cau** (which is written **caw**).

In addition y occurs as an alternative vowel symbol for ie.

1 before the suffix **-ing**, as in *tie, tying*.
2 In words where *two letters* precede the vowel symbol. Thus lie (with *one letter* before the vowel), but try (with *two letters* before the vowel) and shy (with *two letters*, despite the fact that they form one symbol, before the vowel).

Vowel sounds and symbols compared

The most frequently used vowel symbols are listed below.
Sometimes few words belong to a spelling pattern and are
better learned as individual items (for example – *people*,
friend, *pretty*); with other patterns the number of words
which behave in a similar way make it worth providing a
list for children as reference material to be used in the
course of their writing.

sound	symbol	words which exemplify symbols
short a	a	at, cat, that
	a + ve	have
short e	e	pet, met, spell
	a + e marker	ate
	ai	said
	a	any, many
	ie	friend
short i	i	sit, spill, this
	y	lady, baby, happy
	e	pretty
	ee	before, deny { in weakly
		been { stressed
		{ syllables
	u	busy, business
short o	o	hot, shop,
	o + e marker	gone, shone, scone
	-ow	knowledge
short u	u	up, cup, thumb
	o	mother, come, love
	ou	double
long ah	a, ah	pa, ma, ah
	a + th, ss, f	path, father, pass, after
	a + l	alms, half
	a + ff	chaff
	a + sp, st, sk	rasp, mast, mask
	a + r	star
	a + re	are
	ear	heart

sound	symbol	words which exemplify symbols
caw	-all	all, fall, call
	-alt	halt, malt
	-ald	bald
	-aw	law
	-au	cause
long o	o	no, go, so, photo
	o + l	old, cold
	o + e marker	note, bone
	-oe	toe
	oa	boat, goal
	ow, ou	low, grow, know, shoulder
	ew (rare)	shew, sew
long e	e	be, me, we (in grammatical words)
	e + e marker	mete (few examples of this pattern)
	ee	meet
	ea	meat
	ey	key
	ay	quay
	ie	field
	i	litre, India, radii, meridian, idiot
ow	ow	how, now, brown, cow, allow
	ou	out, about, shout
oi	oi	oil
	oy	boy
short oo	u	put (frequently used but rare pattern)
	oo	look
	ou	could
	u + ll	bull, pull, full
long oo	oo	food
	ou	you, souvenir
	oe	shoe, canoe
	ew	flew, new, knew
	ue, u	blue, true, truly
	-wo	two

sound	symbol	words which exemplify symbols
long a	a	angel, able, acorn
	a + e marker	made
	ea	great, steak
	ay	play
	ai	paid
	eigh	eight, weight, neigh, sleigh
long i	i + e marker } y + e marker }	like, type
	ie,	tie
	y	cycle, try, by, my
	i	radii
	i + g	sign
	i + gh	sight
	ei + gh	height
	i + ld	wild, child, mild
	i + nd	hind, mind, find, kind, bind, rind, wind
	I	I
	eye	eye
	aye	aye
short schwa	-er, -or	father, mother, doctor, motor
(see note on effect of weak stress for further examples)		
long schwa	er, ir, ur	her, fir, bird, birth, fur,
	ear	earth, learn
glides from long e to		
short schwa	ere	here
	ear	hear
from short e to	ere	there
short schwa	air	hair
	ear	pear, wear
	are	mare
from short oo	oor	poor
to short schwa	ure	sure
from long i	ire	fire
to short schwa	yre	tyre
	[iro-	ironing]

Words with vowel symbols -ou-, -ow-, -ea- and -ear-

1 **ou, ow** represents six sounds.
a) The most frequent representation is:
ou: loud, cloud, bounce, found, count.
ow: cow, how, now, allow, owl, down.
b) In the following words **ou, ow** represent the long **o** sound.
ou: mould, soul, boulder, shoulder, smoulder, moult, poultry, and a few others.
ow: bowl, bowler, own, below, blow, bow, crow, flow, glow, grow, know, low, mow, row, sow, show, slow, snow, stow, throw, tow, borrow, furrow, pillow, yellow.
c) In the following words **ou** represents the **oo** sound: soup, group, troupe, wound, you, youth, coupon souvenir, trousseau.
d) In the following words **ou** represents the short **u** sound: double, trouble, couple, country, cousin, southern, touch, young, Douglas.
e) In the following words **ou** represents the short **oo** sound: could, should, would.
f) **ow** represents the short **o** sound In *knowledge.*

2 **-ea**, and **-ear**, have seven pronunciations.
a) **-ea** in sea is the main pronunciation.
b) **-ea** in bread has about 60 words of which the following are the most important: *bread, head, dead, dread, instead, spread, lead, read, thread, tread, ready, already, steady, breath, death, feather, leather, heather, health, wealth, stealth, jealous, realm, dealt, peasant, pheasant, pleasant, pleasure, measure, treasure, sweat, sweater, threat, threaten, heaven, heavy, dreamt, leant, meant, leapt, breakfast, breast, cleanse, cleanliness, deaf, treachery, weapon.*
c) **ea** in **great**: *great, steak, yea.*
d) **-ear** in **clear** and also: *ear, dear, fear, gear, hear, near, rear, spear, tear, year, appear, dreary, weary, beard.*
e) **-ear** in **pear** and also: *bear, tear, wear.*
f) **-ear** in **earth** and also: *earl, early, earn, heard, learn, pearl, search.*
g) **-ear** in **heart** and also: *hearth, hearken.*

Grammatical inflections

In a large number of words final **-s, -es** and final **-ed** are used to convey grammatical information. Again these grammatical suffixes remain visually constant although their corresponding spoken forms vary.

-s, -es are used to indicate

> noun plurals in all regular nouns.
>
> noun possessives (which add the apostrophe to indicate singular and plural forms).
>
> third person singular, present tense, indicative mood of weak verbs.
>
> contractions (which add the apostrophe to indicate omission), e.g. *it's* for *it is*, *he's* for *he is*.

1 **-s**, represents **s**, when it occurs in words following the voiceless consonants **p, t, ck, th, f**, for example in *sips, cats, packs, months, biffs.*

2 **-s**, represents **z**, when it occurs in words following the voiced consonants **b, d, g, m, n, ng, -th, v, l**, following vowels and vowels + **r**, for example in *rubs, birds, brags, stems, stains, stings, selves, writhes, fills, shows, furs.*

3 **-es** represents **iz**, when it occurs in all other cases; that is following the consonants **s, z, sh, ch, tch, ge, dge**. For example in *boxes, kisses, raises, mazes, fishes, churches, urges, edges.*

However, in a number of lexical words, although final **s** occurs, it is *not* inflectional. For example: **s** represents **s** in *bus, circus, famous, serious*. But **s** represents **z** in *Mrs, lens, Thames.*

-ed is used to indicate the past participle and past tense of verbs

1 **-ed** represents **t**, which occurs in words following all voiceless consonants except **t**, for example in *skipped, picked, puffed, passed, fished, watched.*

2 **-ed** represents **d**, which occurs in words following all voiced consonants except **d**, following vowels and vowels + **r**, for example, in *grabbed, wagged, slammed, joined, called, banged, waged, tried, stirred.*

3 **-ed** represents **id**, which occurs in words following the consonants **t, d**, for example in *shouted, waded.*

Marker symbols[1]

> The chief function of a *marker* is not that of representing a sound (or other element of the language) but of providing special information about the way another symbol represents a sound.

Vowel markers

> A large number of words is involved in the marking devices which indicate long and short vowel representations for the simple vowel symbols **a, e, i, o, u**:

1 In monosyllabic words of CVC structure with the exception of certain words which always have doubled final consonants (*hill, miss, ruff, egg, add*) a single consonant after the vowel marks the short sound representation: e.g. mat.

2 When suffixes such as **-ing** are added, a double consonant marks the short vowel representation (e.g. matting).

3 The long vowel representation is marked by the addition of a final **e** (in contrast to a second consonant which would mark the short vowel representation) (mate, matt).

4 When suffixes such as **-ing** are added, a single consonant marks the long vowel representation (e.g. mating) and a double consonant (or two different consonants) the short vowel representation (e.g.: netting, nesting).

Consonant Markers

1 The sound representation of symbol **c**, except when it is final in words of more than one syllable, is marked by:

a) **e, i, y**, when it represents the **s** sound in **c**ell, **c**ity, **cy**cle.

b) **a, o, u** and any consonant, when it represents the **k** sound in **c**at, **c**ot, **c**ut, **c**lip. On the addition of a suffix like **-able** when the dropping of the final **e** would mean that **c** represented the **k** sound, the final **e** is retained, as in tra**c**e, tra**c**eable (compare: tra**c**kable).

c) **k** when it is final in a monosyllabic word and its derivatives – as in ba**c**k, stri**c**ken, and when **c** would be followed by a suffix beginning with **i** as in picni**c**king.

2 In words in which the final syllable is formed of syllabic **l** or syllabic **r**, a final **e** is used to mark this – e.g. ab**le**, og**re** (in bub**ble** and bi**ble** the doubled consonants preceding syllabic **l** mark the short vowel representation and the single consonant the long vowel representation).

3 Final **e** is used to mark **g** so that it represents the soft **g** sound as in a**ge**, Geor**ge**. The final **e** is retained when suffixes beginning with **a** are added (mana**ge**, mana**ge**able). In sin**ge** the **e** is retained, whatever form the word takes, so as to differentiate it from sing – e.g. singing, sin**ge**ing. The doubled form of **g** (with soft **g** sound representiation) is **dg**. When this is final in a word it is marked with **e** as in e**dge**.

4 Final **e** is used to mark final **-th** when it represents the voiced sound as in then, thus – ba**th**, ba**the**. In this case the final **e** is a *double marker*, marking both the consonant symbol **th** and the vowel symbol **a**. (Note also **e** as a double marker in ga**ve** and a single marker in gi**ve**).

5 **u** and **h** are used to mark **g** when it represents the hard **g** sound in **g**uest, **g**host, **g**uilt. In words in which **-gu** would otherwise be final, **e** is added – as in va**gue**, catalo**gue**.

6 In lexical words which would otherwise be written with two *letters*, a final **e** is added so as to uphold the rule that *lexical words must be written with at least three letters*. For example toe, see, tie; in *shy*, *fly*, it is the fact that two letters are written that is important – whether these are one symbol (as in the case of *shy*) or not.

7 In certain words which would otherwise end in a non-plural **s**, **e** is added to avoid giving the appearance of plurals (e.g. goose, mouse, noise, praise, else, eclipse, sense, horse). The following are exceptions: *lens, summons, us, his*.

Bibliography

1 WEIR, RUTH H. and VENEZKY, R. L. 'Rules to aid in the teaching of reading', final report, Cooperative Research Project No. 2584, Stanford University, 1965.

2 ALBROW, K. H., The English Writing system: Notes towards a description, unpublished monograph.

APPENDIX 2

The speech sounds of southern British English

Consonant Sounds

A full list of consonant sounds contains 24 such sounds. In the following list of written words the consonant to be sounded is marked in **bold** type:

1 **b**ig	13 **s**it
2 **c**an, **k**ite, **qu**een, ba**ck**	14 **t**op
3 **d**ad	15 **v**an
4 **f**riend, **ph**oto	16 **w**ent, **wh**ere
5 **g**o	17 **y**es
6 ha**pp**y	18 fi**zz**, hi**s**
7 en**j**oy, **G**eor**ge**	19 **ch**ip
8 **l**ook	20 **sh**ip
9 **m**u**m**	21 **th**ing
10 **n**ot	22 **th**en
11 **p**icture	23 mea**s**ure
12 **r**ed	24 si**ng**

Voiced and voiceless consonants

The following table sets out those consonant sounds in which the vocal cords are vibrated (*voiced* consonants) and those in which the vocal cords are silent (*voiceless* consonants). There are eight pairs of consonants which differ only in this respect:

voiced consonants	voiceless consonants
b	p
d	t
g	c (in **c**at)
v	f
j (also g, ge, dge)	ch, tch
z	s (in **s**it)
s (in mea**s**ure)	sh
th (in **th**en)	th (in **th**in)
l, m, n, r, w, y, ng	h

Vowel Sounds

1 the short **a** sound as in **b**a**d**
2 the long **a** sound as in m**a**de, m**ai**d
3 the long **ah** sound as in **ah**, f**a**ther
4 the short **e** sound as in b**e**d, br**ea**d
5 the long **e** sound as in t**ea**cher, sl**ee**p
6 the short **i** sound as in b**i**g, bab**y**
7 the long **i** sound as in l**i**ke, ch**i**ld, **eye**
8 the short **o** sound as in h**o**t
9 the long **o** sound as in h**o**me, b**oa**t
10 the short **oo** sound as in g**oo**d, f**oo**t
11 the long **oo** sound as in m**oo**n, wh**o**
12 the short **u** sound as in m**u**m, c**u**p
   The long **u** sound as in **u**se, l**u**te
   is an alternative way of writing the **oo** sound
   we have already listed, but with or without the
   consonant **y** as in **y**es preceding the **oo**. Thus we
   might write **yooz** for **use**.
13 the short neutral vowel sound as in **a**bove: this is
   not to be confused with the short **a** in c**a**t
14 the long neutral vowel sound as in b**i**rd, h**e**rd, w**o**rd
   (see **schwa**, page 184)
15 the **aw** sound as in f**a**ll, c**aw**
16 the **ow** sound as in h**ow**, l**ou**d
17 the **oi** sound as in b**oy**, b**oi**l
The final three sounds are diphthongs which have the
short schwa preceeded by the short **i**, the short **e** or the
   short **oo**:
18 short **i** + short schwa as in f**ear**, s**eer**
19 short **e** + short schwa as in p**ear**, f**air**
20 short **oo** + short schwa as in p**oor**, t**our**
Note: long **i** + short schwa as in f**ire**, **ir**oning may be
the speech of some speakers while others vary this with
the long **ah** sound: **fire** = **fah**, **ir**oning = **ahning**.

The most frequent consonant sounds

The most frequent consonant sounds in colloquial
southern British English account for 32% of the total.
In order of frequency they are:
   n as in **n**ip
   t as in **t**ip

d as in **d**ip
s as in **s**ip
l as in **l**ip
th as in **then** (*NOT* as in **thin**)

These sounds are also used in high frequency *grammatical items* such as:

n in **n**ot, take**n**, ki**n**dness
t in fishe**t**
d in calle**d**, shoute**d**
s in cat**s**, hit**s**, it**s**, it'**s**
l in **l**ove**l**y, chora**l**,
th in **th**is, **th**at, **th**em, **th**en, **th**ough

(In some lexical words **-th** is spelt **-the**; compare **cloth**, **clothe**; **bath**, **bathe**.)

The most frequent vowel sounds

The Effect of Stress

While they are talking, all native speakers of English use patterns of strong and weak beats. Strong beats (or strong stresses) occur on the syllables of words to which the speaker chooses to give particular meaning. His remaining words or syllables will be weakly stressed and often spoken very rapidly. Thus, in 'How do you do?' (pronounced *How* d'yuh *do*) the first word *how* and the last word *do* may each receive a strong beat (strong stress) and the other syllables (*do* and *you*) then receive weak beats (weak stress). Contrast this with the utterance 'How *do* you *do* it' in which strong stress is placed on both examples of *do* and weak stress on *how*, *you* and *it*. Note that variations of strong and weak stress enable us to distinguish differences of meaning between words such as **content** – meaning that which is contained as in
    'the contents of this box' and
content – meaning satisfied as in 'he was content with his job'.
Similarly strong and weak stress may distinguish **pres**ent and pre**sent**, **pro**duce and pro**duce**, **frequ**ent and fre**quent**.

In spoken English a high proportion of syllables is weakly stressed. The two vowel sounds most commonly found in

southern British English occur in weakly stressed syllables. They are:

1 **Schwa** (or the short neutral vowel) occurs in the following words: about, central, mother, acre, impossible,
   doctor, oblige, colour, and suppose, in colloquial speech.

In addition, this sound may occur in such words as
a, the, to, for, and, do, has, have, of, that, them, there,
was, when these words (they are all *grammatical* words
in that they have little 'meaning' compared with words
such as *picture* and *skipping* which are *lexical* words) are
unaccented. In the following examples the representations of **schwa** are in bold type:

   as big as a house
   she said that we could go out to play
   here and there there were wild flowers growing
   how do you do?
   I gave them back when she asked me to
   They went for a walk
   Where have you been?
   Ask him if he has another pencil for me

In written language, syllables and words have *one
constant spelling* whatever the form they have in rapid
speech. *Therefore the orthography has no single way of
representing schwa.* As seen in the examples above it
may be spelt with most vowel symbols. In this way the
reader is provided with a *single visual* form. The choice
of an appropriate spoken form is left to him.

Reading aloud also requires us to select the appropriate spoken form in order that the correct meaning
of the text is conveyed to the listener.

If teachers are unaware of this difference between the
written and spoken forms of such words, some difficulties affecting the early stages of learning to read and
write are likely to arise. For example, it is not unusual
for children to be taught only the pronunciation appropriate to the strong forms of these words and this
makes reading aloud sound stilted and unnatural. In
learning to write these words it is essential for children
to be able to relate the various spoken forms, which they
already possess, to one written form. This is especially
true of the words *of* and *have* which are pronounced
alike when weakly stressed.

2 The short **i** occurs in the following words:
    baby, needed, manage, indeed orange.
This sound (unlike **schwa**) also occurs in stressed
syllables, as for instance in si**t**, instant, women.
*These two speech sounds – the schwa and the short i
account for almost 20% of all the sounds of colloquial
southern British English speech.*

Spoken and written syllables

A spoken syllable is the result of the way we breathe
and the way our speech organs make sounds. As we
breathe out in speech, the air stream is released in
pulses. These may be long or short, strong or weak,
loud or quiet, slow or fast and they may be accompanied
by a wide difference in pitch between one syllable or
part of a syllable, and another.

Syllables are made up of two elements – consonants
which restrict the passage of air, and vowels which
allow air to pass freely out of the vocal tract. The vowel
is the centre of the syllable – the nucleus which carries
the pulse. The consonants are the outer parts of the
syllable, its beginning and end.

The production of a spoken syllable has three
phases:
1 A chest-pulse pushes a small quantity of air up from the
lungs to the vocal chords.
2 This air passes through the vocal chords.
3 The air passes out of the nose or mouth and a further
air flow is momentarily shut off. Most frequently, however, phase three – the stop placed on the syllable –
coincides with the beginning of a new syllable.
Phase 1 is associated with consonants.
Phase 2 is associated with vowels.
Phase 3 is associated with consonants.

All syllables require the presence of a vowel or a
vowel-like quality. (The existence of *mm* and *sh* are
undoubtedly examples of syllables without vowel
sounds, but they are exceptional.)
1 A few syllables are made up of one vowel sound only,
for example, in certain exclamations Ah! Oh! and in
the words I, a. In words like **airy**, **o**pen, **or**gan, **a**phis,

emu, any, the first syllable of each word consists of a vowel sound only.

2 A large number of syllables is formed by starting with a restricted air flow which is then released – in other words the syllable consists of a consonant or a cluster of consonants followed by a vowel. For example: **into, the, no, die, re**fer, **she, they, through, three, spray**. Such syllables, without a final consonant, are known as *open syllables*.

3 It is also common to find syllables in which the opening or starting consonant is not present, but in which the vowel is followed by a closing consonant or a cluster of consonants. For example **in, out, of, it** and eigh**th**.

4 A very large number of syllables is formed by the presence of all these phases, that is they start with a consonant or cluster of consonants, continue with a vowel and are stopped by a consonant or cluster of consonants. For example: *sit, silt, sings, stings, strings*.

If we write C for consonant (and CC, or CCC for a cluster of consonants) and V for vowel we may express the syllables thus:

```
1    V  )
2  C V  }  open syllables
3    V C )
4  C V C }  closed syllables
```

Initial and final consonants in monosyllables

Not all consonant sounds are permitted at the start of a syllable. For instance the **ng** sound closing the syllable **sing** is only permitted to be in closing or final position in English. In some other languages this is not so – for example, in Chinese (Cantonese dialect). The chief examples of consonants in written words are listed below:

starting or initial consonant in written words		closing or final consonant in written words
C	**V**	**C**
b	any English	b
c	vowel symbol	c
d		d
f		g¹
g¹		ge
h		dge
j or g²		m
k		n
l		p
m		s
n		t
p		(v), ve
r		x
s		ck
t		ff
v		ll
w		ss
y		zz
z		sh
sh		th
th		the
ch		ch
wh		tch
qu		ng
blank		blank

g¹ as in **go**   g² as in **gin**

Consonant clusters

The structure of a syllable, in addition to the features already mentioned on pp. 183–6 may have up to three consonants in a cluster in the initial position and up to four consonants in the final position. When the order of these permitted consonants is set out, they show very obvious patterning, and a different set of restrictions for initial and final positions. For example: *stray* has an initial cluster of CCC, and *acts* has a final cluster of CCC.

Initial clusters of two consonants symbols (CC—)

b + l as in black
c + l as in clap
f + l as in flap
g + l as in glad
p + l as in play
s + l as in slap

b + r as in brown
c + r as in crown
ch + r as in Christmas
d + r as in dress
f + r as in fresh
g + r as in grow
p + r as in print
sh + r as in shrill
th + r as in three

d + w as in dwell
g + w as in Gwen
s + w as in swell
t + w as in twin

s + c, k, ch as in scan, skill, school

s + m as in small

s + l as in slip

s + n as in snow

s + p as in spot

s + t as in stop

Chief final clusters of two consonant symbols (—CC)

l + b as in bulb
l + k as in milk
l + d as in held
l + f as in Alf
l + m as in film
l + n as in kiln
l + p as in help
l + se as in false
l + t as in hilt
l + ve as in delve
l + th as in wealth
l + sh as in Welsh
l + ch as in mulch

b + s as in ribs
ck + s as in backs
ff + s as in puffs
g + s as in rags
ll + s as in hills
m + s as in rams
n + s as in tens
p + s as in tops
t + s as in fits
ng + s as in sings
th + s as in maths
c + t as in act
l + t as in felt
f + t as in left
n + t as in bent
p + t as in apt
s + t as in fist

s + p as in asp
m + p as in lamp

n + d as in and
n + k as in bank
s + k as in ask
t + le as in little

Chief initial clusters of three consonant symbols (CCC—)

$$s \left.\begin{matrix} \\ \\ \end{matrix}\right\} + \left.\begin{matrix} p \\ t \\ c^1 \end{matrix}\right\} + \left.\begin{matrix} r \\ l \end{matrix}\right\} \text{ as in } \begin{matrix} \text{sprint} \\ \text{splay} \\ \text{string} \\ \text{scream} \end{matrix}$$

Chief final clusters of three consonant symbols (—CCC)

These include all syllables which take inflectional **s** without forming an additional syllable, for example: *bulbs, helps (eighths* = **t** + **th** + **s**).

APPENDIX 3

Bibliography of first readers

In the bibliography which follows we have listed some of the primers which make a break with the past. Some are already used in schools, and we suggest that as wide a variety of these as possible should be available in every class of five-year-olds. Sometimes we have listed only a few books from an extensive series.

BAKEWELL, Ruth, *and others, Ready, Steady Rhythm Readers,* W. and R. Holmes, Glasgow, 1965.
   Sky, Bells, Eggs.
An uneven series: the three books listed above are bright and interesting.
BERG, Leila, *Nippers,* Macmillan, 1968.
   Finding a Key, The Jumble Sale, A Day Out, Fish and Chips for Supper.
The first four books of a widely discussed series. Illustrations, though uneven, are excellent at best and indistinguishable from the picture story book quality. Thematically rooted in the real life of most children they provoke discussion and comment from Infants. Later books in the series may be read to the children.
BRUNA, Dick, *I can read,* Methuen, 1968.
A simple text illustrated in Bruna's distinctive style.
CLARK, Mollie, *Looking at words,* Rupert Hart-Davis, 1964.
   5 People we Know, 7 The House, 10 Shops.
An excellent idea – of which these titles are good examples.
COATES, Doreen, *The Yellow Door Series,* Methuen, 1966.
   1 *Painting the Fence,* 2 *The Yellow Door,* 3 *The Birthday Surprise,* 4 *Hide and Seek,* 5 *Feeding the Ducks,* 6 *Katie Gets Lost.*
These are attractive middle-class stories with slightly more difficult texts.
Early I Can Read Books and *I Can Read Books.* World's Work.
HOFF, Syd, *Albert the Albatross, Come and Have Fun, Sammy the Seal.*

HEILBRONN, Joan, *This is the House Where Jack Lives.*
LOBEL, Arnold. *Lucille.*
These are good examples of a new kind of publication half-way between story books and primers. There are many books of this type now available: teachers should exercise care in choosing only the better examples. Some of these books are also included in Appendix 4.
JONES, Clive, *The Jenny and Simon Stories*, Methuen, 1966.
  Jenny's One and Only Cat, The Peacock, Jenny and the Bantam Hen, The Rat Hunt, The Foal, Simon's Rabbit.
The series follows a family who move to the country. The text is fairly hard, the illustrations very attractive. The series continues with a further six books.
McCULLAGH, Sheila, *Griffin Readers*, E. J. Arnold, Leeds, (N.D.).
  The Three Pirates, The Blue Pirate Sails, Roderick the Red, Gregory the Green, The Storm, The Three Pirates Meet.
The beginning of a well known series. More advanced than other books on this list. Attractive to look at and popular with children.
McCULLAGH, Sheila K., *One, Two, Three and Away*, Rupert Hart-Davis, 1964.
  1 *The Village with Three Corners*, 2 *The Haystack*, 4 *The Two Giants.*
A little more difficult. The series deals with a village. Most attractive presentation.
MELSER, June, *Read It Yourself Books*, Methuen, 1966.
  Set A: 1 *What is little?* 2 *What is big?* 3 *What goes fast?* 4 *What comes down?* 5 *What can jump?* 6 *What goes up?* 7 *What goes round and round?*
Poor illustrations but an otherwise outstanding series.
  Set B: 1 *What I like (for boys)*, 2 *What I like (for girls)*, 3 *Where shall I hide?* 4 *Where do you live?* 5 *Which are you?* 6 *What I can do.*
This is the most successful part of the series. These books originate in New Zealand and are not used as extensively in the United Kingdom as deserved.
New Colour Photo Books, E. J. Arnold, Leeds (N.D.).
  First Zoo Book, Second Zoo Book, Toys, More Toys, On the Farm, In the Town, At Home, Games.
Colour photos, usually with single word labels.
PIERS, Helen, *Mouse Books*, Methuen, 1966.
  Mouse Looks for a House, Mouse Looks for a Friend, How did it Happen?
Three excellent books. Attractive substantial format and coloured photographic illustrations.

PIERS, Helen, *The Helen Piers Animal Books*, Methuen, 1968.
Hullabaloo for Owl, Fox and Hen, Goose laid an Egg, What Can Monkey do Next?
Slightly harder than the same author's *Mouse Books* – a charming and witty series.
RANDELL, Beverley and FRIEBOE, Conrad. *Methuen Caption Books*, Methuen, 1966.
Red Books: *At School, The Road, A Birthday Book, Dinner Time.*
The illustrations are undistinguished, the text a repeated sentence pattern.
Yellow Books: *Susan Drew Herself, Susan Drew a House, Peter Drew a Boat, Peter Drew a Train.*
Excellent cumulative texts. Childlike drawings.
Blue Books: *Who are you at the Zoo? Where are you going?*
Who Likes Flies? Where are the Children?
The illustrations are uniform with the Red Books; the text a repeated question and answer form.
Green Books: *A chair is for sitting, A fire is hot, My doll's house, Shopping.*
Illustrations as for the Red Books. The text uses oppositions, questions and deals with the use of everyday articles.
RANDELL, Beverley and McDONALD, Jill. *Methuen Caption Books*, Methuen, 1968.
Purple Books: *A Street, Pockets, Putting Away, Pairs.*
Orange Books: *Funny fishes, Something missing, The rock pool, Boats.*
Recent additions to the series. Jill McDonald's illustrations (see *Methuen Number-Story Caption Books*) combine simplicity and formal excellence.
RANDELL, Beverley and McDONALD, Jill. *Methuen Number-Story Caption Books*.
Set A: *Huge and Tiny, High and Low, Too Large and Too Small, Over and Under.*
Set B: *Less and Less, Fewer and Fewer, Heavier and Heavier,*
An outstanding series which aims to teach number concepts. The eight books are excellent as readers and the illustrations, though only in black and white and a single colour, are simple and successful.
Ready to Read. Schools Publications Branch, Department of Education, New Zealand, 1966.
Early in the Morning, Grandma Comes to Stay, The Fire Engine, Where is Timothy? Going to School, Playtime.
Interesting, sometimes difficult text, with not so attractive 'primerish' illustrations.

Christmas Shopping, Saturday Morning, Painting the Shed, A Country School, The Pet Show, At the Camp.
Harder texts with more successful illustrations.
SOUTHGATE, Vera, *First Words*, Macmillan, 1968.
  Martin's Toys, Jill's Toys, Martin and Jill, Boys and Girls, People, School, Dogs, Pets, In the Country, The Street, Clothes, Colours.
Simple labelled illustrations. Useful as earliest-stage reference books.
TAYLOR, Jenny and INGLEBY, Terry. *This is the Way I Go*, Longman, 1965.
  I Run, I Fly, I Jump, I Crawl, I Climb, I Swim.
An outstanding series. Bright modish illustrations. Each book deals with those creatures associated with the movement of the title.
TAYLOR, Jenny and INGLEBY, Terry, *Stories Around Us*, Longman, 1967.
  Conkers, Fishing, The Lost Puppy, A Home for the Swallows, The New Baby, The Big Blue Diesel, Poor Tired Tim, Philip Takes his Test.
Attractive little books which attempt to follow children's interests.
TAYLOR, Jenny and INGLEBY, Terry. *Reading with Rhythm*, Longman, 1961.
  Set 1: *Tommy's Engine, The Little Kettle, The Woo-Wind, Soup for Dinner.*
  Set 2: *The Old Kettle, Snip-Snip and Snap, Rag Doll Nancy, King Lion.*
  Set 3: *David's Birthday, Careless Caroline, The Little Key, The Clock on the Wall.*
TAYLOR, Jenny and INGLEBY, Terry. *Read by Reading*, Longman, 1964.
  Set 1: *The Three Wicked Goats, The Hero, The Treasure, I Will Do Battle.*
  Set 2: *Granny's Three Black Cats, Amanda's Magic Mirror, The Weatherman, If I Had a Lot of Money.*
  Set 3: *Simon's Zoo, The Four Young Swans, Borriquito's Story, Zarifa the Young Camel.*
Imaginative text with attractive illustrations. Fairly advanced.
WILLIAMSON, Alice, *Gay Colour Books*, E. J. Arnold, Leeds.
  1 *The Little Blue Jug*, 2 *The Little Yellow Duck*, 3 *The Little Orange Top*, 4 *The Little Green Hat*, 5 *The Big Red Ball*, 6 *The Little Black Cat.*

APPENDIX 4

Bibliography of nursery rhyme books

Selected and annotated by Nicholas Tucker

BRIGGS, Raymond. *Fee, fi, fo, fum*, H. Hamilton, 1964, Penguin Books, 1969.
Ring-a-ring o'roses, H. Hamilton, 1962.
The White Land, H. Hamilton, 1963.
The Mother Goose Treasury, H. Hamilton, 1966. In this book, Raymond Briggs turns away from the more leisurely tone of his earlier three anthologies, and crams 408 rhymes into half as many pages. Many of these rhymes are the more traditional tough versions that have been dug out by Mr and Mrs Opie, and Raymond Briggs' illustrations match these in vigour and occasional crudity. An excellent anthology for boys!
HALEY, Gail. *One, Two, buckle my shoe*. A Book of Counting Rhymes. World's Work, 1965.
LINES, Kathleen. *Lavender's Blue*. Illustrated by Harold Jones. O.U.P., 1954. A modern classic, slightly old-fashioned in its appeal, but with immense atmosphere, and wide selection of rhymes.
MONTGOMERIE, Norah. *This little pig went to market*, illustrated by Margery Gill, Bodley Head, 1966. A really comprehensive collection of play rhymes, with instructions, mostly for the very young.
Nursery rhymes for certain times, illustrated by Elinor Darwin and Moyra Leathem, introduced by Walter de la Mare, Faber, 1956. Includes many of the older rhymes.
OPIE, Iona and Peter. *The Oxford Nursery Rhyme book*, O.U.P., 1955. Easily the most comprehensive collection of nursery rhymes ever made, and illustrated wherever possible by original woodcuts from largely eighteenth century sources. An invaluable source book.
The Puffin Book of Nursery Rhymes, Penguin Books, 1963. An ingenious selection, grouped so that one theme leads on to another, and with some very readable annotations at the end.
POTTER, Beatrix. *Appley Dapply's Nursery Rhymes*, F. Warne. *Cecily Parsley's Nursery Rhymes*, F. Warne. Some traditional

and new rhymes, illustrated with familiar Beatrix Potter characters. The small size of these books helps make them especially popular with younger children.

REEVES, James. *The Merry-go-round*, illustrated by John Mackay, Heinemann, 1955, Puffin Books, 1967. A collection of traditional rhymes and poetry from all possible sources, to suit every mood of children from five to ten.

SPIER, Peter. *London Bridge is falling down*, 1968, World's Work.

To Market! To Market!, 1968, World's Work. Each book illustrates one or just a few nursery rhymes, using fascinating detail often drawn from original historical sources.

WILDSMITH, Brian. *Mother Goose*, 1964, O.U.P. A very colourful collection, each rhyme clearly set out on its own page.

APPENDIX 5

Bibliography of picture story books

ALIKI. *My Hands*. A and C Black, 1967. (Let's read-and-find-out Science Books.)
Gaily illustrated simple text on different uses for hands.
AMBRUS, Victor. *The Three Poor Tailors*, O.U.P., 1965.
Simple retelling of a Hungarian folk tale of the three poor tailors who ride to town on a goat, and the hilarious misadventures that befall them. Vigorous illustrations in rich colour. Won the Kate Greenaway Medal in 1966.
ARDIZZONE, Edward. *Little Tim and the Brave Sea Captain*. O.U.P., 1955.
Little Tim stows away and is involved in a drama at sea. A little boy's dream-come-true story with self-explanatory illustrations.
BARTLETT, Margaret Farrington. *Where the Brook Begins*. A and C Black, 1964. (Let's read-and-find-out series.) Illustrated by Aldrea A. Watson.
Well written very simple text that really does explain where and how the brook begins.
BEMELMANS, Ludwig. *Madeleine*. Deutsch, 1952.
Madeleine, a little French schoolgirl, has her appendix out. Simple rhyming text, charming illustrations with Parisian backgrounds. The first of a series of Madeleine books.
BIRO, Val. *Gumdrop: the adventures of a vintage car*. Brockhampton Press, 1966.
How an Austin Clifton Twelve-Four gradually disintegrates and is then happily restored to win a prize in the Beaulieu Rally. Text reads aloud well; excellent details of the parts of the car, and pictures that more or less tell their own story.
BLAKE, Quentin. *Patrick*. Jonathan Cape, 1968.
Patrick's violin makes many magical things happen: fish fly, cows colour and dance, pipes puff fireworks and birds sprout bright new feathers. A most charming book.
BLAKELY, Peggy. *Colours*. A and C Black, 1966, illus. Philippe Thomas.
Probably the best of the *Things I Like* series. Useful for discussion with children.

also: *Fast and Slow, Shapes, Fur and Feather, Big and Little, Sounds.*

BONSALL, Crosby Newell. *Who's a Pest?* World's Work. 1963. (An I can read Book.)

Homer draws moustaches on his sisters' dolls, and is called a pest. He sets out to prove that he is not and is involved in a great deal of hilarious word play. The witty illustrations can be enjoyed in their own right.

BROOK, L. Leslie. *Johnny Crow's Garden.* Warne, 1950.

A classic which still retains its vigour and gaiety. The text is ideally simple; the illustrations, though dated, are charming.

BRUNA, Dick. *The School.* Methuen, 1966.

A day at school for the very young. Simple text, and attractive stylised pictures.

Tilly and Tessa. Methuen, 1959.

Twins aged three who have their fourth birthday party. Attractive stylised pictures in primary colours. Tough format.

BUCKLEY, Helen E. *Grandfather and I.* World's Work, 1962, illus. Paul Galdone.

Little boy goes walking with his grandfather and compares walking with him with other members of the family.

Grandmother and I. World's Work, 1962. Illus. Paul Galdone.

Grandmother's lap and the laps of the rest of the family and what a little girl feels when she's sitting on them. Simple text, charming illustrations.

BURNINGHAM, John. *Humbert, Mr Firkin and the Lord Mayor of London.* Cape, 1965.

How Humbert, humble horse of Mr Firkin, scrap-iron merchant, rises to dizzy heights in the Lord Mayor's show. Excellent text for reading aloud.

also: *Borka: the adventures of the goose with no feathers.* (Kate Greenaway Medal winner, 1964.)

Trubloff: the mouse who wanted to play the balalaika. Cape, 1964.

BURTON, Virginia Lee. *The Little House.* Faber, 1964.

How the countryside round the little house develops through the decades until it is the centre of a large American city, and how finally the little house is happy again. Delightful textual layout and very attractive pictures. Caldecott Medal winner.

Mike Mulligan and His Steam Shovel. Faber, 1942.

Progress catches up on Mary Anne, the steam shovel, but Mike Mulligan and the people of Popperville find a way to save her from the scrap-heap. Lively text for reading aloud, gay informative illustrations.

also: *Choo, Choo: the story of a little engine who ran away.* Faber, 1956.

CHAPMAN, Gayner. *The Luck Child*. Hamish Hamilton Ltd., 1968.
Based on a story by the Brothers Grimm and boldly illustrated in bright colours.

CHAUCER, Geoffrey. *Chanticleer and the Fox*, adapted and illustrated by Barbara Cooney. Longman Young Books, 1960.
Delightful realisation of the story for reading aloud. Beautiful illustrations. Won the Caldecott Medal (awarded by the American Library Association for illustration) in 1959.

DE REGNIERS, Beatrice Schenk. *May I Bring a Friend?*, illus. Beni Montressor. Collins, 1966.
The King and Queen issue invitations to various occasions and each time 'I' asks to bring a friend, who are animals of all sorts. Simple rhyming texts, highly original illustrations in very with-it colours. Won the Caldecott Medal in 1965.

ETS, Marie Hall. *In the Forest*. Faber, 1955.
A little boy goes for a walk in the forest and calls all his animals to a party until Dad comes to take him home to bed. Delightful, simple text for reading aloud. Black and white illustrations.

ETS, Marie Hall. *The Fox Went Out One Chilly Night*. World's Work, 1962.
An old song enchantingly illustrated by Peter Spier. The music is also included.

FOREMAN, Michael. *The Great Sleigh Robbery*. Hamish Hamilton, 1968.
A modish story of the robbing of Santa Claus foiled by the action of all the children of the world. Very trendy, very successful and deservedly popular. May be familiar from the cartoon version shown on television.

GAG, Wanda. *Millions of Cats*. Faber, 1953.
The very old man sets out to find a cat to cheer himself and his wife. Charming story, simple text, stylised black and white illustrations. A picture story book classic.
also: *Snippy and Snappy*, *ABC Bunny*, *The Funny Thing*, *Gone is Gone*, and others.

GOODALL, John S. *The Adventures of Paddy Pork*. Macmillan, 1968.
Black and white illustrations and a most original use of half-sized pages dramatically carry the story. There are no words and children will want to verbalise the tale.

GRAMATSKY, Hardie. *Little Toot on the Thames*. World's Work, 1965.

New York harbour tug boat is accidentally towed across
the Atlantic and has adventures on the Thames. Gay text
for reading aloud. Lively illustrations with London backgrounds.
also: *Little Toot*. World's Work, 1951.
HERMANN, Frank. *The Giant Alexander*. Methuen, 1964.
A gentle giant helps people in trouble – and cleans Nelson's
column with his toothbrush. Text for reading aloud, delightful self-explanatory pictures.
also: *Giant Alexander and the Circus*. Methuen, 1966.
HEWITT, Anita. *Mrs Mopple's Washing Line*, illus. Robert
Broomfield. Bodley Head, 1966.
The wind blows Mrs Mopple's washing all over the farmyard
and festoons the animals. Clear illustrations which tell their
own story; text for reading aloud.
HUTCHINS, Pat. *Rosie's Walk*. The Bodley Head, 1968.
A simple story told in thirty-two words, wittily complicated
by a visual sub-plot. Rosie seems to be totally unaware of
the fox's constantly foiled attacks. This book has been widely
used to stimulate discussion.
HUGHES, Shirley. *Lucy and Tom's Day*. Gollancz, 1965.
An ordinary day for two pre-school children with simple
present tense text and excellent illustrations of everyday
people and happenings.
KEATS, Ezra Jack. *Whistle for Willie*. The Bodley Head, 1964.
Peter learns to whistle for his dog. This is the second most
popular in the series by a distinguished American illustrator.
also: *The Snowy Day*, The Bodley Head. (Caldecott Medal
1963) *Peter's Chair*.
KEEPING, Charles. *Charley, Charlotte and the Golden Canary*.
O.U.P., 1967.
Charley misses his friend Charlotte who has moved to a
high block of flats. In brilliant colour Keeping captures much
of the essence of urban life today. A dazzling book.
also: *Alfie and the Ferryboat*. O.U.P., 1968.
KORNITZER, Margaret. *Mr Fairweather and his Family*, illus.
Margery Gill. Bodley Head, 1960.
Simple, well told, story of the adoption of a baby, in fact
two babies, giving the facts of adoption very clearly, and
stressing the love that Mr and Mrs Fairweather want to
give to their new babies. The author is editor of *Child
Adoption*.
KRASILOVSKY, Phyllis. *The Cow Who Fell in the Canal*, illus.
Peter Spier, World's Work, 1958.
Hendrika the Dutch cow who longs for adventure, which
she has in abundance when she falls in the canal. Text reads

aloud very well. Charming detailed illustration with Dutch background.

The Very Little Girl, illus. Ninon. World's Work, 1959.
A little girl who is smaller than all sorts of usual things, then grows bigger and is compared again with all sorts of usual things. Charming simple text, plenty of attractive illustrations showing size relationships.

KRUSS, James. *3 × 3: Three by Three*. illus. Eva Johanna Rubin, transl. Geoffrey Strachan. Methuen, 1965.
Three mice, three cats, three foxes, etc., chase in and out of the mouse house. Vivid bold illustrations, excellent memorable rhyming text.

LA FONTAINE, *The Lion and the Rat*, illus. Brian Wildsmith. O.U.P.
Glorious illustrations to the simply told fable.
also: *The Hare and the Tortoise*. O.U.P., 1966. *The North Wind and the Sun*. O.U.P., 1964. *The Rich Man and the Shoemaker*. O.U.P., 1965.

LANGSTAFF, John. *Frog went-a-courting*, illus. Feodor Royankovsky. World's Work, 1961.
Vivid, gay illustrations to the old song, the tune is included. A Caldecott Medal winner.

LEAF, Munro. *The Story of Ferdinand*, illus. Robert Lawson. Hamilton, 1955. Penguin Books.
The reluctant bull who loved flowers more than fighting. Bold black and white illustrations.

LENSKI, Lois. *The Little Farm*. O.U.P., 1944.
Farmer Small and his day around the farm. Very simple. Clear stylised illustrations.
also: *Davy's Day*. O.U.P., 1945. *Debbie and her Grandma*. O.U.P., 1968.

LIONNI, Leo. *Inch by Inch*. Dennis Dobson, 1968.
Collage illustrations tell the story of the caterpillar forced, on the threat of being eaten, to measure the birds.

LOBEL, Arnold. *The Bears of the Air*. World's Work, 1966.
Four endearing bottle-nosed bears prove to grandfather that his text-book on bear behaviour is out of date.

MACDONALD, Golden and WEISGARD, Leonard. *The Little Island*. Cambridge, 1959.
A beautiful picture book with simple poetic text telling of the island through the seasons, its plants, animals and the seas around it.

MAYNE, William. *The House on Fairmount*. Hamish Hamilton, 1968, ilius. Fritz Wegner.
Magic in suburbia. At No. 1965, Fairmount Avenue (a vacant lot) a strange house appears and is found to be made of sweets.

NESS, Evaline. *Mr Miacca*. Bodley Head, 1967.
A most moral tale about a bogey man.
PERRAULT, Charles. *Puss in Boots*. Bodley Head, 1968, illus.
Barry Wilkinson.
A gay and grand version of the story. Both this and the
Benn edition (illustrated by Hans Fischer) are worth having.
also: *Tom Thumb*, illus. by Wilkinson, 1967. *Lazy Jack*, illus.
by Wilkinson, 1969.
PIATTI, Celestino. *The Happy Owls*. Benn, 1965.
The owls try, without success, to pass on their secret of
happiness to the barnyard fowls. The translated text is a
little flat, but the illustrations are glorious, like stained
glass.
also: *The Holy Night*, The Bodley Head, 1968.
POTTER, Beatrix. *The Tale of Peter Rabbit*. Warne, 1902.
Perennially fresh story. Animal observation in the illustrations is superb.
REY, H. A. *Zozo*. Chatto and Windus, 1956.
The gay pictures tell the story of the monkey who was too
curious. One of a popular series.
ROSE, Elizabeth. *How St Francis Tamed the Wolf*, illus.
Gerald Rose. Faber, 1958.
Gay retelling of the legend with a fairy tale ending. Vivid
expressive illustrations.
The Magic Suit (retold from the story by Hans Andersen),
illus. Gerald Rose. Faber, 1966.
Lively realisation of the Emperor's Clothes. Vivid, very
funny illustrations.
also: *St George and the Fiery Dragon*. Faber, 1963. *Old Winkle
and the Seagulls*. Faber, (Kate Greenaway Medal winner).
SENDAK, Maurice. *Where the Wild Things Are*. Bodley Head,
1967.
Max sails away to the land where he is king of the wild
things – and when he gets back his supper is still hot. The
wild things are very weird but Max is in full control all the
time. Distinctive illustrations that need the story to explain
them. (Caldecott Medal, 1964.)
also: *Hector Protector and As I Went Over the Water*.
SEUSS, Dr. *The Cat in the Hat*. Collins, 1961. (I can read
all by myself Beginners Book.)
Cartoon-like illustrations. Cleverly rhyming text.
also: *One fish, Two fish, Red fish, Blue fish*. Collins and Harvill,
1962.
SLOBODKIN, Esphyr. *Caps for Sale: a tale of a pedlar, some
monkeys and their monkey business*. World's Work, 1959.
Simple illustrations which tell their own funny story.

SPIER, Peter. *London Bridge is Falling Down*. World's Work, 1968.
A most charming book that small children delight in reading and re-reading. Not to be missed.
also: *To Market! To Market! And So My Garden Grows. Hurrah, We're Outward Bound.*
STOBBS, William. *The Three Billy Goats Gruff*. The Bodley Head.
Lively gouache illustrations to the traditional tale. The troll is half giant-aphid, half dalek.
also: *Henny Penny. A Frog He Would A-wooing go.*
TOLSTOY, Alexei. *The Great Big Enormous Turnip*. Heinemann, 1968, illus. Helen Oxenbury.
A familiar tale with 'mod' illustrations.
UNGERER, Tomi. *The Three Robbers*. Methuen, 1961.
The three robbers are converted by orphan Tiffany to do good works. Witty, bold illustrations.
also: *Moonman*, Whiting and Wheaton, 1966. *Crictor*, Methuen.
WILDSMITH, Brian. *Wild Animals*. O.U.P., 1967.
An outstandingly beautiful book. Destined to be a classic picture book. Wildsmith won the Kate Greenaway Medal in 1963 for his ABC.
also: *Fishes*. O.U.P., 1968. *Birds*. O.U.P., 1967.
WILL and NICHOLAS. *Finders Keepers*. World's Work, 1964.
Nap and Winkle, two delightful mongrels find one bone and try to find someone to arbitrate between them. In the end, of course, they share it. Vivid bold illustrations. A Caldecott Medal winner.
ZEMACH, Harve. *The Speckled Hen*. The Bodley Head, 1967, illus. Margo Zemach.
Full of life and wit a Russian nursery rhyme adapted and illustrated in a vigorous fashion.
ZION, Gene. *Harry, the Dirty Dog*, illus. Margaret Bloy Graham. Bodley Head, 1960. Penguin Books, 1968.
Harry, an endearing mongrel, escapes from being bathed and gets as dirty as he can, but finally he has to beg for a bath so that his family can recognise him again. Vividly detailed pictures.

APPENDIX 6

Bibliography of books for the teacher

The Medium

DIACK, H. *In Spite of the Alphabet*, Chatto and Windus, London, 1965.

DOWNING, J. A. *The Initial Teaching Alphabet Explained and Illustrated*, Cassell, London, 1964.

SCEATS, John. *i.t.a. and the Teaching of Literacy*, Bodley Head, London, 1967.

GATTEGNO, C. *Words in Colour*, Background and Principles, Education Explorers, Reading, 1962.

JONES, J. K. *Colour Story Reading*, Nelson, London, 1967.

STERN, C. and GOULD, T. S. *Children Discover Reading*, Harrap, London, 1966.

STOTT, D. H. *Roads to Literacy*, Holmes, Glasgow, 1964.

The Message

GODDARD, Nora L. *Reading in the Modern Infants' School*, University of London Press, 3rd edition, 1969.

LEE, Doris M. and ALLEN, R. V. *Learning to Read through Experience*, Meredith Publishing Co., 1963.

WARNER, Ashton, Sylvia. *Teacher*, Penguin Books, 1966. (See also: *Spinster* and *Myself* by the same author.)

Theory and practice examined

CENTRAL ADVISORY COUNCIL FOR EDUCATION (ENGLAND). *Children and Their Primary Schools*, H.M.S.O., 1967.

HUEY, Edmund Burke. *The Psychology and Pedagogy of Reading*, Foreword by John B. Carroll. The M.I.T. Press. Paperback edition 1968.

GOODACRE, E. J. *Reading in Infant Classes*, N.F.E.R., 1967.

MORRIS, Joyce M. *Standards of Progress in Reading*, N.F.E.R., 1966.

Reading in the Primary School, N.F.E.R., 1959.

MORRIS, R. *Success and Failure in Learning to Read*, Oldbourne, 1965.

REID, Jessie F. Learning to Think about Reading, in *Educational Research*, 9 No. 1, pp. 56–62, published for N.F.E.R. by Newnes Publishing Co. Ltd.

Linguistics, Reading and Spelling

DURKIN, D. *Phonics and the Teaching of Reading*, Teachers College Press, Teachers College, Columbia University, 1966.
GOODMAN, Kenneth S. and FLEMING, James T. (eds). *Psycholinguistics and the Teaching of Reading*, The International Reading Association, Delaware, U.S.A., 1969.
LEFEVRE, Carl A. *Linguistics and the Teaching of Reading*, McGraw-Hill, 1964.
PETERS, Margaret L. *Spelling: Caught or Taught?* Routledge and Kegan Paul, 1967.

Phonetics and Linguistics

ABERCROMBIE, David. *Elements of General Phonetics*, Edinburgh University Press, 1967.
BROWN, Roger. *Words and Things*, The Free Press of Glencoe, 1958.
HALL, Robert A. *Linguistics and your Language*, Doubleday, New York, 1960.
LAMB, Pose. *Linguistics in Proper Perspective*, Charles E. Merrill Publishing Company, Columbus, Ohio, 1967.
HALLIDAY, M. A. K., McINTOSH, Angus and STREVENS, Peter. *The Linguistic Sciences and Language Teaching*. Longman, 1965.
VENEZKY, Richard L. The Structure of English Orthography. The Hague: Mouton and Co., 1969.

For Parents and Teachers

COLLINS, J. *Improving your Baby's Intelligence*, National Society for Mentally Handicapped Children, 230 Ormeau Road, Belfast, BT 72 F2, 1969.
GREEN, Lawrence, *Parents and Teachers – Partners or Rivals*. George Allen and Unwin, 1968.
YOUNG, Michael and McGEENEY, Patrick. *Learning begins at Home. A study of a Junior School and its Parents*, with a foreword by Lady Plowden, Routledge and Kegan Paul, 1968.

APPENDIX 7

Schools which participated in the trial of Breakthrough to Literacy materials

Miss E. Swann,
Elswick Road Infants'
  School,
Elswick Road,
Newcastle upon Tyne

Mrs M. R. Carter,
Wharrier Street
  Infants' School,
Wharrier Street,
Newcastle upon Tyne,
NE6 3EY

Miss H. Ladyman,
Montagu Infants' School,
Moor View Crescent,
Montagu Estate,
Newcastle upon Tyne

Mr J. C. C. Nutman,
Gosforth C.P. School,
Archibald Street,
Gosforth,
Newcastle upon Tyne 3,
NE3 1EB

Miss J. Simpson,
Coxlodge C.P. Infants'
  School,
Wansbeck Road South,
Coxlodge,
Gosforth,
Newcastle upon Tyne,
NE3 3PE

Mrs A. Nutman,
Gosforth C.P. School,
Hartford Road,
Gosforth,
Newcastle upon Tyne 3,
NE3 5JQ

Miss M. E. Crow,
Woodlands Park C.P.
  School,
Canterbury Way,
Woodlands Park,
Wideopen,
Newcastle upon Tyne 3

Miss M. Sykes,
Berry Brow C.P. School,
Birch Road,
Berry Brow,
Huddersfield,
HD4 7LP

Mrs D. Robinson,
Mount Pleasant C.P.
  School,
Mount Street,
Lockwood,
Huddersfield

Miss G. E. Marsh,
Reinwood County
  Infants' School,
Burfitts Road,
Oakes,
Huddersfield

Mr D. S. Sinclair,
Clapgate County J. & I.
  School,
Cranmore Drive,
Leeds 10

Mr N. H. Green,
Holy Trinity C. of E. J. &
  I. School,
Green Lane,
Cookridge,
Leeds 16

Miss B. Lewis,
Ingram Road C.P.
  Infants' School,
Brown Lane,
Leeds 11

Miss M. A. Smith,
Osmondthorpe C.P.
  Infants' School,
Wykebeck Avenue,
Leeds 9

Miss D. G. Lloyd,
Littleham County
  Infants' School,
Exmouth,
Devon

Mr G. M. Williams,
Withycombe Raleigh
  C. of E. School,
Exmouth,
Devon

Mr D. Cooke,
Marpool County
  Primary School,
Exmouth,
Devon

Mrs E. Bradley,
East Allington Primary
  School,
East Allington,
Totnes,
Devon

Miss A. Hillman,
Penwerris C.P. School,
Stratton Terrace,
Falmouth,
Cornwall

Mr E. W. Lever,
St Erth C.P. School,
Hayle,
Cornwall

Miss D. S. Lloyd,
Romney Avenue
  Infants' School,
Horfield,
Bristol 7

Miss D. Earp,
Shirehampton Infants'
  School,
Springfield Avenue,
Shirehampton,
Bristol

Mrs W. K. Griffiths,
Filton Avenue Infants'
  School,
Lockleaze Road,
Horfield,
Bristol 7

Mrs I. M. Icke,
Hall Green Infants'
  School,
Stratford Road,
Birmingham 28

Mr R. E. Frankish,
Lozells Junior and
  Infant School,
Gerrard Street,
Birmingham 19

Miss D. M. Walton,
Percy Shurmer Infants'
  School,
Sherbourne Road,
Birmingham 12

Mrs D. D. R. Glass,
Yardley Wood Infants'
  School,
School Road,
Birmingham 14

Mr R. D. Worton,
Oakham Junior and
  Infant School,
City Road,

Tividale,
Warley,
Worcs.

Mr C. C. Brown,
Tividale Hall Junior &
  Infant School,
Regent Road,
Tividale,
Warley,
Worcs.

Mr B. E. Willetts,
Tividale Junior and
  Infant School,
Dudley Road West,
Tividale,
Warley,
Worcs.

Miss F. Collinson,
Alkrington County
  Infant School,
Manor Road,
Alkrington,
Middleton,
Manchester,
M24 1JZ

Mrs Ullock,
Askham Infants' County
  School,
Dalton in Furness,
Lancashire

Mrs E. Lyon,
St George's C. E.
  Infants' School,
Schools Street,
Tyldesley,
Manchester

Miss H. Woodward,
Bowerham Infants'
  School,
Bowerham Road,
Lancaster

Mrs M. R. Bates,
Cranborne Infants'
  School,
Birchwood Avenue,
Hatfield,
Herts.

Miss F. M. Knowles,
Lionel School,
Lionel Road,
Brentford,
Middx.

Miss H. Rothschild,
Canonbury Infants'
  School,
Canonbury Road,
London N.1

Miss D. M. Whiteside,
Wilberforce Infants'
  School,
Herries Street,
Kilburn Lane,
London W.10

Sister M. Joan,
St Anne's Junior Mixed
  School,
Underwood Road,
London E.1

Mrs Woolley,
Selincourt Primary
  School,
Selincourt Road,
London S.W.17

Miss B. E. Robbins,
Hungerford Infants'
  School,
Hungerford Road,
York Way,
London N.1

Mr Cleaver,
Wedgewood Primary
  School,
Marinefield Road,
Langford Road,
Fulham,
London S.W.6

Miss Griffiths,
Wandsworth Training
  Centre,
9 Spencer Park,
S.W.15

INDEX

printed vocabulary in Sentence
Maker, 93–5
Programme in Linguistics and
English Teaching, v–viii
progress,
rates of for *Breakthrough to Literacy*,
2;
marking, 3;
recording, 55–7

psychology and the teaching of
reading, 79
punctuation, 36–7, 155

reading aloud,
by the children, 46–7;
by the teacher, 43, 62–3
reading, skills involved, 82–3
recording progress,
see progress
remedial reading,
reasons for failure, 81–2, 153;
use of *Breakthrough to Literacy*, 149–61
restrictions in children's writing,
107–9

Sentence Maker – children's model,
in remedial reading, 150–4
integration with other materials,
59, 61;
introduction and use in the
classroom, 18–29;
re-use of, 28–9;
stages in learning to use, 23–6, 95–8;
theory underlying design and use, 3,
90–102;
what to do when it is complete, 27–9
Sentence Maker – teacher's model,
integration with other materials, 58,
60;
introduction and use, 8, 14–17;
specimen lessons with, 72–3
storage, 9
specimen lessons,
see lesson plans
speech and writing,

changes in, 121
major differences between, 118–20,
135–6;
misconceptions about, 122–4
speech sounds of Southern British
English, 181–5
spelling,
adding inflections with Sentence
Makers, 26;
and the Word Makers, 103–6;
history, 121
opinions of English spelling, 115–17;
place of spelling, 33–6;
rules of English spelling, 131–40,
164–90
spelling games, 31–2, 35–6, 61
Stern, Catherine, 78
storage of materials, 9–12
stories,
see picture story books
Stott, D. H., 78
stress
effect of, 183–5;
excluded from writing system, 117
syllabic writing systems, 113
syllables, 185–90
symbols, 30, 102, 104–5, 128–31,
164–80, 187–90

testing,
see progress, marking

vocabulary in Sentence Maker,
see printed vocabulary
vowel sounds, 182–5
vowel symbols, 128, 168–77

Warner, Sylvia Ashton, 92
whole word method, 88, 138
Word Maker, 30–8;
and remedial teaching, 160;
directions for making teacher's
model, 71;
integration with other materials, 59,
61;